art & crafts for KiDS

THE AUSTRALIAN **Women's Weekly**

about the book

The importance of art and craft projects for children cannot be overestimated. Creative play stimulates even the youngest child's imagination and, upon completion of the project, promotes a great sense of achievement.

This book features brilliant step-by-step projects that kids and adults will love. Where preparation is required, it is simple and fast and, if the project is particularly messy, we've included advice on cleaning up. The content is best suited to younger children, aged from two to eight. Older children may use their enthusiasm to take simple projects further, without the need for constant adult supervision.

The projects have been chosen to assist children in the growth of many skills, including concentration, small muscle development, hand-eye coordination, sensory discrimination, problem-solving and decision-making.

Ideal for parents, grandparents, teachers, play-group supervisors and those who train teachers, this book will provide all carers with good ideas and the means to carry them out. Kids will never be bored during school holidays again!

Most importantly, though, you should use this book to help develop your child's confidence and pride in his or her own ideas. If a child is inclined to copy what he or she sees in the photographs in this book, put the book out of sight. Encourage children to experiment – they need to know there is no one right way for their art to look when finished. Self-expression should be fun!

contents

guidelines & equipment

Every preschool, kindergarten, community group or family where young children are involved in arts and crafts will need certain basic items. Look for supplies at variety and discount shops. However, when quality and safety are important, as with scissors, buy items in shops specialising in these requirements. Don't overlook though, the endless variety of materials found in nature that can be used for art and craft projects.

 Age: we have suggested a minimum age for most projects as a guide to projects that may prove too difficult for younger children. ALL AGES means from two years upwards but these projects still require supervision. The ages given are a guide only, as children differ in their ability to master certain steps. With close supervision, younger children may be able to manage more difficult projects, although their attention span may not last until the project is finished. We have used the word 'adult' to show where help will be needed for very young children, or where toxic products or sharp instruments are to be used, or where cooking or heating is required.

basic items

Adhesive tape: invest in a heavy tape dispenser which is easy for children to use.

Brushes: should be at least 1½cm (⁵⁄₈in) wide and have long handles (over 15cm [6in]). Occasionally fine-pointed brushes are needed for a particular project. Brushes should be cleaned in cold water and soap after use, and stored in a can with their bristles up or wrapped in newspaper. Provide a brush for each paint colour; if the brush has a coloured handle, match it with the paint colour to encourage children to return the brush to the original paint bowl.

Coloured chalk: avoid hard, scratchy chalk. Soft, brightly coloured chalk is relatively inexpensive and available from art and craft supplies stores.

Crayons: should be at least 13mm (½in) in diameter for children under five to use.

Small thin crayons break easily and are difficult for little fingers to grip. Child-care experts suggest breaking the crayons to overcome the child's apprehension of breaking them. Remove some of the wrapper to encourage full use.

Fabric crayons: are available from art and craft supplies stores. Designs must be heat-sealed according to the manufacturer's instructions.

Felt-tipped pens: are available in many colours. Ensure the pens are non-toxic. Also look for thick felt pens which are easier for small hands to grip.

Foil: any type of foil such as aluminium foil or tin foil can be used.

Glitter: easiest to use in a coarse salt shaker. Put a sheet of newspaper under the project. Shake the excess glitter onto the newspaper. Lift each side so that the glitter falls to the fold in the newspaper. Put one end of the fold onto the edge of the open salt shaker and lift paper to allow glitter to fall into shaker.

Needles: can be used by children over five years but they should be blunt and have a large eye, such as a darning needle. When threading a needle, the end of the string must be stiff so children can push it through the needle hole easily. This can be done by either wrapping a piece of sticky tape around the end of the string or by dunking the end in melted wax and leaving it to set. When weaving wool, adhesive tape can be wrapped around the end of the wool to stiffen it as an alternative to using a needle.

Newsprint paper: is cheap and comes in colours. It absorbs liquid more than other paper and tears more easily. Ideal for easel painting. Available from printers' supplies shops.

Oil pastels: smooth and vividly coloured, they give the effect of oily chalk.

Paint rollers: use rollers as an alternative to paintbrushes.

Papier-mâché: a technique where pulped paper soaked in **paper paste** is moulded into shapes, or where objects are covered with strips of paper dipped into paper paste and then left to dry.

Plaster bandage: these are gauze bandages impregnated with plaster and available from chemists. To use, just wet the bandage and place over a mould. They dry quickly and are great for making masks and sculpture.

Plasticine: available in many colours. It can sometimes be hard for little hands to manipulate, especially in cold weather.

Scissors: cheap scissors are a waste of money because soon they will not cut without tearing. Spend a little more money on small scissors with a blunt end. Left-handed scissors are available at art and craft supplies stores.

Staplers: use medium-sized staplers, about 10cm (4in) to 15cm (6in), because purse-sized staplers break easily and large staplers are too difficult for children to press down.

paste & glues

Clear craft glue: more expensive than **PVA glue** and not as strong, although it's faster drying. It is particularly helpful in holding fabrics and laces in place, but will seep through fabrics if applied too liberally. It is harmful if eaten or inhaled.

Commercial liquid starch: can be purchased already made up in many stores. It has an indefinite storage life.

Commercial paper paste: any sort will do but the most vivid colours are achieved with paper paste made for lightweight wallpapers, hobbies and crafts. Follow the directions using cold water and stir briskly while adding the powder and for a minute afterwards. It often has lumps at first, but these usually disappear in a few hours. Commercial paper paste has no fungicide, is non-toxic and lasts for several days in an airtight container.

Cornflour paste: (see page 8).

Extra strong homemade liquid starch: (see page 8).

Flour paste: (see page 8).

Homemade commercial-strength liquid starch: (see page 8).

Paper paste: cornflour paste or flour paste (see recipes page 8) can be used for papier-mâché or collage. **Commercial paper paste** is widely available.

PVA glue: stands for poly vinyl adhesive and is widely available.

Starch: (see page 8).

paint

When the type of paint is not specified but listed as 'paint', any sort of non-toxic paint will do. Always store in an airtight container. Have children wear aprons while painting and keep a bucket of soapy water and sponges on hand.

Fabric paint: is available from art, craft and department stores. Use when permanent prints on fabric are required. **Fabric crayons** can be used to draw designs directly onto fabric.

Fingerpaint: any thick non-toxic paint can be used for fingerpainting. Fingerpaint can be made by adding powder paint, food colouring, vegetable dye or tempera paint to cornflour paste (see recipe page 8).

Food colouring: widely available in liquid form from supermarkets. It can be used as a substitute for vegetable dye, but the colours are paler. Food colouring also comes in a paste which is more intense in colour, but is more difficult to find.

Painting on foil and plastic: mix ½ cup of thick **powder paint** mixture with 1 teaspoon of dishwashing liquid. If the paint does not adhere, add another ½ teaspoon of dishwashing liquid. The dishwashing liquid makes the paint stick to glossy surfaces.

Powder paint: available in a variety of colours. Powder paint is an economical paint that is mixed with water. **Cornflour paste** can be added to the mixture to achieve a thicker consistency.

Powder tempera paint: available in a large variety of colours as a powder and also as a liquid. It is a flat opaque paint which is better suited for some art projects as it covers writing on boxes very well. Put powder in a container, add a little water to make a paste then add a little more to make paint. Liquid starch, **cornflour paste** or **paper paste** can be added to give it transparency and to increase volume as it can be expensive. It may rub off onto hands and clothing when dry. Thick paint sometimes cracks but adding paper paste helps to prevent this.

Thick paint: powder paint or **vegetable dye paint** can be mixed with cornflour to create a thicker consistency.

Thin paint: powder paint or **vegetable dye paint** can be diluted with water to create a thinner consistency.

Vegetable dye: is made by placing about 1 tablespoon of water in a container and adding ⅛ of a teaspoon of dye powder and stirring. Add more dye for a more intense colour. Vegetable dye can be purchased at children's educational toy stores. **Food colouring** can be used as a substitute.

Vegetable dye paint: made by dissolving about ⅛ of a teaspoon of **vegetable dye** powder in a tablespoon of water and adding it to **paper paste** or **starch**. The colours are most brilliant and translucent when mixed with commercial paper paste. It does not cover lettering on boxes or newsprint as well as **powder tempera paint**, which is an opaque paint.

unusual painting tools

Refillable roll-on deodorant containers filled with paint.
Feather duster used on a very large sheet of paper as a paintbrush.
Plastic squeeze bottles.
Shaving brushes.
Feathers.
Fly swatter.
Sponges.
End of a piece of cardboard.

printing techniques

Paint is applied to the object to be printed usually by three methods: painting the object with a brush; rolling over the object with a hard paint roller or print roller that has been covered with paint by rolling in a paint-filled tray; or by pressing the object onto a print pad. On page 9 we show you how to make a print pad.

clay

Natural clay is excellent for modelling. It is available from art and craft supplies stores, but buy it in solid form as it is messy to make up from powder. Pieces of clay can be sliced off a block of clay with string or wire tied to two empty thread reels. Interesting textures can be made by scraping or pressing objects into the clay. Children may want to save the clay objects they have moulded. Let the objects dry thoroughly and they can be painted or lacquered and glued onto a wooden base if desired. It is not advisable to fire the clay products of young children as any air bubbles trapped in the clay will explode and someone will be very disappointed. Clay that is to be fired must be kneaded until the air bubbles escape. Clay is a bit messy. The table top can be protected with a heavy garbage bag that has been cut open and taped down. This or any

similar material can be thrown out afterwards. Save all excess clay in an airtight container to prevent it drying out. If storing for more than a few days, press a thumb into each clay ball and fill hole with water. Clay can clog drains so scrape the excess into a storage container. Although the main purpose of clay is manual manipulation, every child should experience the delight of putting it through a garlic press!

collage & construction

Collage is artwork made from various materials glued, taped or stapled to a surface. Assorted collage materials include dyed pasta, chenille sticks (pipe cleaners), cellophane, magazine pages, crepe paper, leaves, flowers, seashells, wood shavings—the list is endless!

Crepe paper curls: cut ½cm (¼in) strips off the end of a roll of crepe paper. Cut through completely one end of strip and roll the strips between your palms to separate the unfolded papers.

how to dye collage materials

Matchsticks, toothpicks, iceblock sticks: place in a warm vegetable dye mixture. Wood colours more quickly in warm dye. Spread on newspaper to dry.

Paper: fill a baking dish with water and add vegetable dye or food colouring. Lay paper flat in the baking dish until completely submerged. Hang paper to dry. For best results use rice paper or a thin absorbent paper.

Pasta: wearing gloves, place food colouring or vegetable dye (start with ⅛ teaspoon) into cold water. Place pasta into the dye, swish it around and remove quickly before it becomes sticky. Spread on a thick wad of newspaper. As it is drying, run your hand over pasta to keep it from adhering to the newspaper.

safety first

Activities that involve small objects, such as polystyrene, beads and buttons should be kept for older children, over five years. There is a high risk that younger children will put these objects into their mouths, ears or noses.

Before buying or using craft materials check labels to ensure that all felt-tipped pens, crayons, play dough, paints and glues are non-toxic. Play dough can be made at home with edible dye (see play dough recipes on page 9).

Supervise children using scissors to avoid cuts and wounds. Make sure all scissors are put away after use. Choose scissors with a blunt end or children's safety scissors or training scissors.

Supervise all use of string and cord so that children do not use it to cut off circulation or breathing.

Older children only should use needles and these should be blunt-ended. Keep pins and needles in a secure container away from children. Make sure all pins and needles are put away after use to avoid nasty accidents.

Supervise all washing up of tools after use. Water is dangerous and children can drown in a small amount of water.

collecting & storing materials

These materials will be handy for collage, construction, painting, printing and many other children's crafts.

bark	confetti	foam pieces	mesh	plastic containers	sticks
beads & buttons	corks	fur	old clean socks	polystyrene pieces	straws
bottle tops	corrugated cardboard	greeting cards	old telephone books	rubber bands	string
boxes & containers	cotton reels	postcards	orange & onion bags	sandpaper	thread
cardboard sheets	cotton wool	hair curlers	paper & cardboard	seeds	wire
cellophane	cylinders	magazines	paper clips	shells	wire coat-hangers
chenille sticks	egg cartons	matchsticks	paper patty pans	springs	wood off-cuts
clock parts	fabric scraps	matchboxes	pasta (dry)	squirt & spray bottles	wool

Store collage and craft materials in separate containers to avoid mixing them up. It can be a nightmare trying to separate hundreds of small items! Make collecting items fun and encourage children to think creatively about how they can expand their collections of collage and craft materials.

fingerpaint & glue recipes

cornflour paste

Add to ordinary paint or add food colouring to use as fingerpaint; use as an economical extender for paint; use as a paper glue or use in papier-mâché.

you will need
3 parts water (3 cups)
1 part cornflour (1 cup)
food colouring
saucepan

1 **Adult:** bring the water to boil in a saucepan. Remove from heat.
2 **Adult:** dissolve cornflour in a little cold water and add to hot water, stirring constantly. Boil until clear and thick (about 1 minute).

To make fingerpaint, add desired food colouring. This mixture will be very smooth. Offer it to the children while it is still warm to touch. A tablespoon of glycerine may be added to make it glossy. A ½ cup of Lux soap flakes may be added to give fingerpaint a lumpy texture.

Store in refrigerator as it spoils in hot weather.

flour paste

Useful for gluing collage and papier-mâché paper.

you will need
1 part water
1 part flour
food colouring
oil of cloves, wintergreen or peppermint
bowl
spoon

1 Pour water into bowl. Add flour, stirring constantly. Add food colouring. Salt may be added for a different texture.
2 Add a few drops of oil of cloves, wintergreen or peppermint as preservatives. Thin with cold water.

Store in airtight container in refrigerator. Longlasting.

starch

Very useful for gluing paper. It dries clear and sticks to glass, metal, waxed paper and plastics. Occasionally commercial-strength liquid starch is not thick enough.

you will need
1 part starch granules (1 cup)
2 parts boiling water (2 cups)
food colouring
saucepan

1 **Adult:** add a small amount of cold water (about 6 tablespoons) to starch granules to make a paste.
2 **Adult:** add boiling water to starch, stirring constantly. The mixture should become thick and milky glossy. If it doesn't thicken it is because the water isn't hot enough. Simply put it on the stove and bring it to the boil. Remove from stove.
3 Add food colouring. Add some glycerine to make mixture glossy and/or ½ cup of Lux soap flakes for a different texture. Give starch mixture to children while still warm.

Store in refrigerator as it spoils in hot weather.

homemade commercial-strength liquid starch
Dissolve 1 teaspoon of granulated starch in a small amount of water. While stirring, add 1 cup of hot water. Bring to the boil for 1 minute, stirring constantly. Cool.

Store in airtight container in refrigerator. Longlasting.

extra strong homemade liquid starch
Follow instructions for homemade commercial-strength liquid starch (above), using 1 tablespoon of granulated starch instead of 1 teaspoon.

play dough recipes

play dough

you will need
1 cup salt
2 cups flour
4 teaspoons cream of tartar
2 tablespoons cooking oil
2 cups water
powder paint or vegetable dye or food colouring
saucepan

1 Mix all ingredients in saucepan.
2 **Adult:** cook on medium heat for 3–5 minutes, stirring constantly until mixture becomes stiff. Store in airtight container in refrigerator. It will last for quite a while and has the consistency of commercially prepared play dough. Additional colour may be worked into dough.

how to make a print pad

you will need
thin sponge
shallow tray

1 Place a sponge in the tray. Place several spoonsful of paint onto the sponge.
2 To print, just press the printing object onto the sponge. The sponge loads a minimum amount of paint, evenly distributed across the printing object, which helps to avoid smearing and gives a clear print. Make a cushion by placing a newspaper under the paper on which the print impression is to be made.

uncooked salt dough

This is the easiest recipe; it can be made in less than 3 minutes. Let children make the dough themselves whenever possible. This recipe makes enough for six children.

you will need
powder paint or vegetable dye or food colouring
2 cups flour
1 cup salt
1 tablespoon cooking oil
1 cup water
bowl
spoons

1 Mix powder paint or vegetable dye or food colouring with the flour and salt. Add oil and water.
2 Knead dough. Children will like to use rollers, biscuit cutters and toothpicks with dough. If it becomes sticky, add more flour. Dough will keep for more than a week, even longer if it is kept in the refrigerator but it has a tendency to crumble.

Small shapes of this mixture can be baked in a 180°C (350°F) oven for 45 minutes to make them hard.

tip   Children will sometimes want to add more flour to play dough to make it seem like they are really bakers. Occasionally, leave the dough white so they can colour it themselves with powder paint in plastic salt shakers. Fragrances may be added to any of the dough mixtures. Let children mix different coloured dough together; this will give a marbled effect. Wash utensils used to make dough before it dries on them. Play dough will clog the drain so don't try to dispose of it by washing it away. Disinfectants and alum are sometimes added as preservatives but they are not necessary in recipes with a high salt content. Salt sometimes attracts moisture if dough is in a sealed container, so if the mixture is sticky, just add a little flour to get the right consistency.

drawing &
painting

Children love the sensations of blending
colour, texture and design. Experimenting with
different types of paint—whether thick, thin,
airy or glossy—or different drawing tools
—wax or chalk crayons, cork, pencils or pens
—can lead children on a sensory adventure.
Encourage experimentation with colours, tools
and designs, and let different techniques be
combined to create delightful new effects.

creating different effects for drawing

Good quality felt-tipped pens give the greatest colour with good clarity of line. Unfortunately, these pens dry out easily, so must be kept capped.

Chalk colours are more vivid if the paper has been dampened with a sponge before drawing. Chalk also dries with more colour and a slight gloss when the paper has been brushed with evaporated milk or buttermilk before using the chalk.

Burnt cork can be used to create a charcoal effect on paper. An adult can burn the end of a long wine cork with a match or lighter. The child then draws on paper with the burnt end of the cork. When the burnt end wears off, the cork can be burnt again.

Coloured pencils, wax crayons and oil pastels are also good drawing tools for children to use.

ideas to stimulate children's imaginations

Children enjoy making drawings from their initials and can produce the most imaginative interpretations. Another idea to inspire individual and original expression is for an adult to scribble on paper and let a young child turn the scribbles into people, animals, or space creatures, for instance. Turning objects upside down and drawing them provides another interesting perspective. Children will more readily try a new interpretation (rather than reproducing the object accurately) if the object is treated differently or becomes unusual.

OVER
3
YEARS

fingerprint drawings

you will need
child's ink pad
sheet of paper
felt-tipped pen

1 Gently place finger on stamp pad so that finger is well-covered with ink. Carefully press finger on paper ensuring that finger does not move and smudge the ink. Allow prints to dry.
2 Draw features on a single print or several fingerprints to make them into creatures, birds, flowers or insects.

magic drawing

OVER
4
YEARS

you will need
liquid bleach
cotton buds
coloured tissue paper or
    white paper painted all
    over with thin paint
sheet of paper
small bowl

1 **Adult:** put about 1 tablespoon of bleach in bowl. Replace bleach lid and put up on shelf out of reach of children.
2 Put end of cotton bud into bleach and then place that end onto tissue paper and draw a picture. Within a few seconds the area that has been touched with bleach will turn a paler colour or white. Darker colours may need more bleach. The disappearance of colour on tissue paper shows up better when a sheet of white paper is placed directly underneath.

Safety first
Ensure that bleach does not come in contact with skin.
Keep lid on bleach and keep it out of reach of children at all times.

Place your magic drawing over white or brightly coloured cardboard or paper to make unusual cards or wrapping paper.

ALL AGES

neighbourhood drawing collage

you will need
sheets of coloured paper
large sheet of paper
felt-tipped pens
glue
scissors

1 Ask children to draw their family
   home, garden, pets, cars and
   family friends on coloured paper.
2 **Adult:** cut out pictures.
3 Glue pictures onto sheet of paper.

A neighbourhood collage is a
great project for a group of
children. Each child can add
the elements that are important
in his or her neighbourhood.
It's a stimulating way for
children to show how they
see their own environment.

blot painting

Apply the paint close to the fold line.

you will need
sheet of paper
paint in small bowls
spoon or paintbrush
apron

1 Put on apron.
2 Fold paper in half. Open it out. Very young
   children will need the paper to be pre-folded.
3 Spoon or brush the paint out in drops onto
   paper, mainly along the central fold line.
4 Re-fold paper. Rub paper with palm of hand
   from fold out to the edge of the paper.

Open out the paper to admire the effect.

Cut a shape out of
the blot painting and
hang it on your wall
as a decoration.

window painting

Powder paint is recommended because it wipes easily off windows and has the most intense colours. Soap paint and any paint mixed with white liquid shoe polish are also suitable. Paste- and starch-based paint is hard to wash off windows.

you will need
newspapers
powder paint mixed in
   small bowls
paintbrushes
adhesive tape
apron

1 Put on apron.
2 Tape newspaper to bottom of window and floor to protect floor and ledges from paint.
3 Paint onto inside of window as rain will wash off any outside painting. Paintings can be left for days or weeks.
4 Wash painting off with sponge and soapy water. The paint does not mark window in any way but the longer it is left, the harder it is to remove as it seems to bake on.

Some window paintings are so pretty you'll wish they'd last forever.

crayon-resist painting

you will need

sheet of paper
crayons
tempera powder paint mixed in
    small bowl
paintbrush
apron

Tempera powder paint gives the most dramatic
result because of its opaque quality.

1 Put on apron.
2 Pressing down firmly, draw a design on the paper
   with different coloured crayons.
3 Cover drawing with the paint. The best results occur
   when light-coloured crayons are used with dark paint
   or dark-coloured crayons are used with light paint.

sponge painting

you will need

small sponge pieces

clothes pegs

paint, small amounts in shallow trays

sheet of paper

apron

1 Put on apron.

2 Hold sponge pieces with a peg.

3 Dip sponge into the paint and use it to dab or brush paint onto the paper making pictures and patterns.

4 Keep the sponge pieces in their original paint tray to avoid mixing colours. It also helps to colour match the peg with the paint, for example, a blue peg with the blue paint, etc.

Repeatedly dabbing the sponge onto the paper can create striking geometrical effects.

Using the sponge as a brush is a great way to colour large spaces.

monster painting

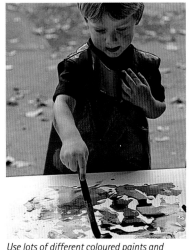

Use lots of different coloured paints and allow them to mix and run together.

you will need

thin paint in small bowls
paintbrushes or rollers
sheet of paper
felt-tipped pens
apron

1 Put on apron.
2 Paint over the paper with several different colours.
3 Allow the colours to mix and run together all over the paper.
4 Hang painting to dry.
5 Ask an adult to help you find monsters in the painting. Outline monsters using a felt-tipped pen.

roller painting

Dab, swirl, circle or drag the roller. What other roller techniques can you think of to use?

you will need
foam rollers, preferably small
thin paint in shallow trays
paper, absorbent not shiny
apron

1 Put on apron.
2 Dip the roller into the paint and spread the paint, trying different techniques, for example, waves or stripes. Repeat with different colours. Encourage children to replace rollers in original colour containers as paint blends quickly.

OVER 2 YEARS

fingerpainting

you will need

fingerpaint (see page 8 for recipe),
1 to 3 colours in bowls
with large spoon
laminated tabletop
grout scrapers (from hardware store)
plastic combs
apron

1 Put on apron.
2 Spoon the fingerpaint onto the tabletop. Spread paint with hands to mix colours and enjoy the sensory experience. Draw patterns and pictures with hands and fingers, moving them all over the tabletop.

An excellent extension activity for older children is to use grout scrapers and combs to make patterns in the paint. Patterns can be made by scraping in straight lines or swirling movements.

There's no need to be too careful when applying the paint before fingerpainting.

Dragging a grout scraper or comb through the paint creates attractive wavy patterns.

cleaning up

Have a large dish of warm, soapy water at the ready for paint-soaked hands. Remove aprons as soon as painting is finished to avoid getting paint on clothing. Some children may be reluctant to use fingerpaint. They may prefer to use a roller to spread the paint and a cautious fingertip to paint patterns. Emphasise that fingerpainting isn't dirty.

body painting

you will need

sheet of paper, larger than
   the child
crayons
paint in small bowls
paintbrushes
scissors
apron

1 Put on apron.
2 Place paper on floor. Child should lie face up on top of paper.
3 Using a crayon, draw an outline around the child's whole body.
4 Colour in body drawn on paper with crayons or paint.
   Older children might like to create a series of characters.
5 Finished figures can be cut out and used for further play.
   This activity encourages development of a positive self-image.

Ask a friend to draw an outline around you.

Use different colours for different body parts.

Carefully cut around the body shape.

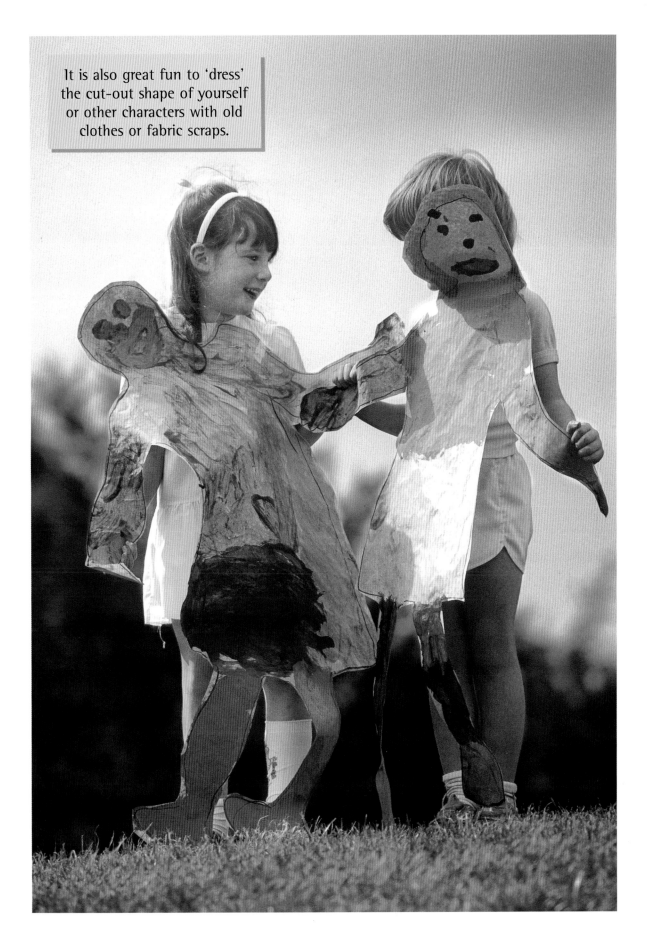

It is also great fun to 'dress' the cut-out shape of yourself or other characters with old clothes or fabric scraps.

ALL AGES

mural painting

you will need

masking tape or bull-dog clips

length of heavyweight paper
(more than 1 metre [1 yard]
wide)—an end roll of
heavyweight paper is often
available, free of charge,
from newspaper publishers
or printers

fence, brick wall or easel

paint in small bowls

paintbrushes

apron

1 **Adult:** tape or clip paper along a fence or a brick wall,
or tape or clip the paper onto an easel.

2 Put on apron. Paint pictures on paper. Mural painting
is a fun group activity, especially at parties.

Make up your own play
and use the mural as
back-drop scenery. Cut
into sections, tape to a
wall and change it each
time for different acts.

spray-paint mural

you will need

masking tape or bull-dog clips
length of heavyweight paper
    (more than 1 metre [1 yard]
    wide)—an end roll of
    heavyweight paper is
    often available, free of
    charge, from newspaper
    publishers or printers
brick wall, fence or easel
thin paint in red, yellow and blue
spray bottles
apron

1 **Adult:** tape or clip paper along
   a fence, a brick wall or tape or
   clip the paper onto an easel.
   Pour paint into spray bottles.
2 Put on apron. Squirt the paint
   onto paper. Colours will mix
   and overlap, creating various
   patterns on the paper.

A spray-paint mural is a colourful party activity and makes a beautiful decoration.

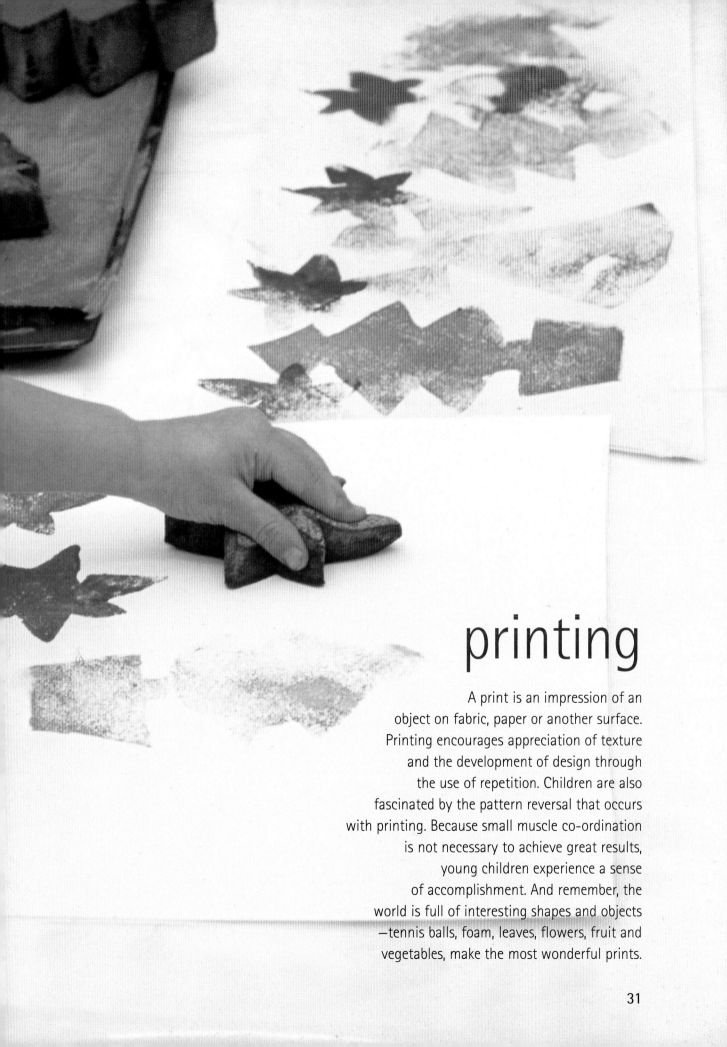

printing

A print is an impression of an object on fabric, paper or another surface. Printing encourages appreciation of texture and the development of design through the use of repetition. Children are also fascinated by the pattern reversal that occurs with printing. Because small muscle co-ordination is not necessary to achieve great results, young children experience a sense of accomplishment. And remember, the world is full of interesting shapes and objects —tennis balls, foam, leaves, flowers, fruit and vegetables, make the most wonderful prints.

fingerpainting prints

you will need
fingerpaint (see page 8)
table top (preferably laminated)
bucket of warm soapy water
large sheet of paper
towel
apron

1 Put on apron.
2 Put a small puddle of fingerpaint onto table top.
3 Fingerpaint on table top. When finished, wash hands in bucket of warm soapy water and dry them thoroughly with the towel.
4 Place a large sheet of paper on top of the fingerpainting. Carefully rub back of paper all over with clean, dry hands. Lift one side of paper print and slowly peel paper print off table top. Hang print up to dry.

Prints can also be made of pictures painted on the table top.

Fingerpainting is wonderful for releasing children's tension and anger while developing their hand-eye co-ordination.

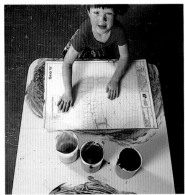
Place paper on fingerpainting, then place hands in the centre of paper and rub hands out to the edges without moving the paper.

fish prints

you will need
fresh dead fish with large scales (flat if possible)
newspaper
thin paint
paintbrush
absorbent paper, cut to size (blotting paper works well)
apron

1 Put on apron.
2 Lay fish on newspaper. Dry the fish with paper towels if it is still damp. Paint one side of fish all over.
3 Carefully place absorbent paper on painted side of fish. With flat, dry hand, press paper onto painted fish, taking care not to move paper. Lift paper off and allow the print to dry. Several prints may be taken each time the fish is painted. The first print is not always successful if there is too much paint on the fish.
4 More colourful results can be achieved by two means. The first is to paint different parts of the fish different colours before applying the paper. The second is to follow steps 1 and 2, then paint the fish a second, different colour and overprint fish onto the first dried print.
tips After a thorough cleaning, the fish is still perfectly good to eat. You can use these same techniques with other types of seafood; prawns give a particularly good result.

Spread the paint evenly over one side of fish.

Make several prints each time fish is painted.

foam prints

you will need
thick foam
paint-loaded
   print pads (see page 9)
paper
scissors
apron

1 **Adult**: using scissors, cut thick foam into shapes. Shapes could be Christmas symbols, Easter eggs, geometric patterns, animals or letters. Older children can cut out their own printing shapes.
2 Put on apron. Press foam shape onto print pad then onto paper to make a print. Continue printing, using different colours and shapes until you are satisfied with the effect.
3 Hang prints to dry. Wash paint from foam shapes.

To make a print, press thick foam shape onto print pad then press foam onto paper.

Use different foam shapes and different colours to create different visual effects.

OVER 3 YEARS

marbling

you will need
large polystyrene trays
waterproof ink, various colours
plastic spoons
light-coloured blotting paper
apron

1 Put on apron.
2 Half fill trays with water and gently spoon small amounts of ink onto surface of water. Stir mixture very carefully and slowly.
3 The ink will float, swirl and ooze to form fascinating patterns.
4 Place blotting paper on top of floating colours for 30 seconds. Quickly lift paper off, turn over, and immediately hold horizontally to stop ink running. Allow paper to dry on a flat surface.

Marbling on thin absorbent paper looks striking taped to a window.

tennis ball prints

Remember to return each tennis ball to the correct bowl so as not to mix the paints.

Dab or roll balls, and if you drop them be careful not to splatter paint everywhere.

you will need
tennis balls (one for each paint colour)
thin paint in shallow bowls
sheet of paper
apron

1 Put on apron.
2 Dip tennis ball in paint. Dab, roll or drop ball on paper to make print.
3 Repeat the process with each different colour. Remember to keep balls in their original paint bowls to avoid mixing colours.
4 Hang or lay the prints flat to dry. If prints are hung, the paint tends to run and adds interesting patterns to the design. If you want clear splatter prints leave the prints to dry on a flat surface.

Use Christmas colours to print festive wrapping paper.

OVER 4 YEARS

foot prints

you will need

paint

large baking dish

heavy sheet of paper
(about 2 metres [about
6½ft] long)

rocks

bucket of water and soap

spoon

towel

1 Using a spoon, spread a
thin layer of paint over the
bottom of the baking dish.

2 Lay paper on grass. Weigh
down its edges with rocks
to stop wind blowing paper.
Place baking dish at one
end of paper and bucket
of water and towel at
other end.

3 Step into baking dish then
walk along paper, making
different patterns. When
at the other end, step into
bucket of water and wash
feet with soap. Dry with
towel. Children may need
to hold someone's hand
while stepping from baking
dish to paper, and from
paper to the bucket.

4 Change colour in baking
dish and repeat. Replace
piece of paper before
painting becomes too wet
and slippery.

note If only lightweight paper
is available or if the paper
tears when it is trodden
on, place paper on a
concrete path.

string block prints

you will need
string or rope
small block of wood
paint in shallow tray (about 1cm [3/8in] deep)
sheet of paper
paintbrush
apron

Wrap the string around the block several times so that interesting lines are formed.

1 Put on apron.
2 Wrap string around wooden block several times (making sure there is not a build up of string in one spot), and tie string in place at top of block.
3 Press string block into paint tray or paint string with paintbrush.
4 Make a print by placing string block on paper and pressing. Move block around in different directions until an interesting print design is created.

OVER 5 YEARS

crayon screen prints

The lines of the design need to be quite thick so draw over the design a couple of times.

Lay the fabric or garment flat and smooth out creases before you place the screen on top.

Ask a friend to hold the screen while you drag the squeegee across the screen surface.

Ask a friend to hold down the fabric or garment while you gently lift the screen.

you will need
oil pastel crayons
silk screen
fabric or garment
  (for printing)
fabric paint
squeegee
cleaning rag
mineral turpentine
spoon
apron

1 Put on apron.
2 Using crayons draw a design directly onto the mesh of the screen.
3 Draw over the design again until the crayon lines are quite thick.
   If printing a garment place paper between front and back to avoid paint
   soaking through both layers of fabric. Place fabric or garment underneath
   the screen and spread fabric so there are no creases. Spoon a thick strip of
   paint along one side of the screen. If using more than one colour, spoon
   strips of paint alongside each other being careful not to overlap the paint.
4 Have an adult or friend hold the screen firmly. Drag the squeegee across
   the screen surface, spreading paint evenly. Repeat two or three times.
5 Have an adult or friend hold the fabric or garment. Carefully lift screen,
   raising it from one side to the other. Remove excess paint from the screen.
6 **Adult:** saturate a rag with mineral turpentine and scrub the crayon
   pattern off the screen. Wash the screen thoroughly with cool water.
7 Hang the fabric or garment to dry. Before wearing or washing, iron the
   fabric (according to paint manufacturer's instructions) to fix the paint.

roller prints

OVER
4
YEARS

you will need

foam shapes, wool, string or tyre
    inner tube
cardboard cylinder
thick paint-loaded print pad
    (see page 9)
large sheet of paper
PVA glue
apron

1 Put on apron.
2 Glue foam shapes, wool, string
   or tyre inner tube around the
   cardboard cylinder.
3 Roll cardboard cylinder onto foam
   print pad. Then roll the cylinder
   over the paper. Repeat the print
   until the paper is covered.

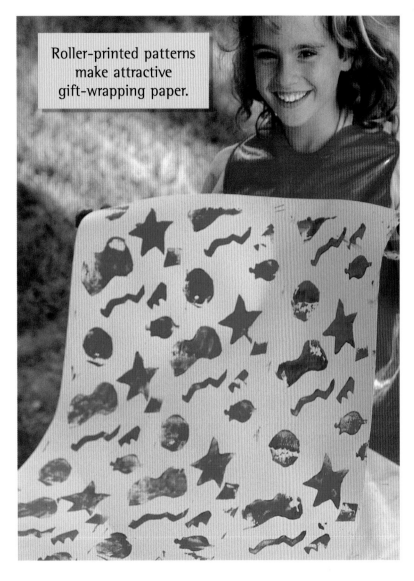

Roller-printed patterns
make attractive
gift-wrapping paper.

*Arrange the foam shapes and objects so that
there is a uniform space between them.*

*Use lots of different shapes to create a
striking visual pattern.*

*Roll the cylinder on the print pad, making sure
the paint evenly coats the shapes.*

*Carefully roll the cardboard cylinder without
rubbing the paint off the shapes.*

printing 41

spool prints

you will need

paint-loaded print pads
(see page 9)
spools of various shapes
and sizes
sheet of paper
apron

1 Put on apron.
2 Press the spool onto print pad,
then press the spool onto paper.
Continue printing using different
spools and different colours.

*Young children will love the feeling of using
spools of different shapes and sizes.*

Glue the spool prints
onto cardboard and
cover with clear self-
adhesive plastic to make
bright placemats.

kitchen gadget prints

you will need

kitchen gadgets such as ice
  block trays, strainers, whisks,
  containers, biscuit cutters, and
  any gadget with an interesting
  shape and a flat surface
paint-loaded print pads
  (see page 9)
large sheets of paper
apron

1 Put on apron.
2 Press printing gadget onto print
   pad. Stamp gadget onto paper to
   make a print. Continue printing
   with different objects and colours
   until the print is complete.

Whisks of all shapes and sizes make great printing gadgets and they're also fun to use.

Try printing on different coloured paper for striking and colourful effects.

printed doll

you will need

printing surface such as a
  laminated board, ceramic tile,
  heavy plastic or thick glass
pencil
fabric paint
paintbrushes
2 pieces of cotton fabric
needle and sewing thread or
  sewing machine
polyester fibre filling
raffia or wool for hair
fabric glue
ribbon
buttons, if desired
felt scraps, if desired
scissors
pins
apron

1 Put on apron.
2 On printing surface, draw a pencil outline of doll so both sides of doll are
  same shape. Paint picture of the front of the doll on the printing surface.
4 Place a fabric piece over the painted design and press gently with an open
  hand. Try not rub the fabric because the paint will smear.
5 Lift the fabric carefully, without moving it sideways. Hang the print to
  dry. Clean and dry the printing surface and paint a back view of the doll.
  Make a second print and leave to dry. Iron both fabric pieces (according
  to the paint manufacturer's instructions) to fix the paint.
6 Place both fabric pieces together and cut out around the doll, leaving
  a 2cm-wide (¾in) allowance. Avoid having very narrow sections of
  fabric as these will be difficult to fill with the fibre.
7 **Adult:** pin the two fabric pieces together with the printed sides to
  the inside. Stitch around the shape with a needle and thread, or sewing
  machine, and using a 2cm-wide (¾in) seam. At the top of the doll, leave
  a 10cm (4in) opening in the stitching to insert the fibre filling.
8 Turn through to right side and fill with fibre filling. Stitch opening closed.
9 Take a length of raffia or wool strands and plait each end, leaving an
  unplaited section in the centre. Glue the unplaited section onto the
  doll's head to make hair, leaving the plaits free. Tie the plaits with ribbon.
  Sew or glue on buttons for eyes and a felt nose, if desired.

Carefully paint within the pencil outline of the doll so that both sides are the same shape.

Ask someone to help you place the fabric over the painting so the print doesn't smudge.

With the palm of your hand, gently press, but do not rub, the fabric onto the painting.

Slowly peel the fabric off the doll painting without lifting the fabric sideways.

Cut around the edge of both doll shapes leaving at least a 2cm-wide (¾in) allowance.

An adult will need to sew the two sides together, then you can add the hair.

dyeing

Dyeing is an easy way to colour fabric. Results are quick, often spectacular and give a sense of satisfaction and accomplishment—a boost to any child's self-esteem. Children love exploring colour blending and discovering new dyeing effects. They'll be thrilled with their results such as wall hangings, tablecloths, cushion covers and T-shirts.

paper dyeing

you will need

various papers, such as rice paper sheets, coffee filter papers, blotting
    papers or paper towels (absorbent paper will give the best results)
food colourings mixed with water, in several bowls
eye droppers
apron

Unusual folds make more interesting pictures.
Experiment with folds to see the effects.

1 Put on apron.
2 Fold the sheets of paper into eighths or sixteenths.
3 Dip a corner of folded paper into a colour then remove.
4 Dip another corner into a second colour then remove.
5 Repeat with all corners of folded paper. Unfold and dry.

For variation, use eye droppers to create a colourful design
on the paper (in this case, there's no need to fold the paper).

Dip a corner of folded paper into one colour.

Then dip another corner into a second colour.

Repeat with all corners, using many colours.

Fill eye dropper with colour from one bowl and drop spots of colour onto the paper.

Use another eye dropper to add a second colour and allow the colours to blend.

OVER
6
YEARS

dip & dye

you will need

2 or 3 vegetable dyes or cold-water fabric dyes
2 or 3 buckets or large ice-cream containers
cotton fabric
rubber gloves
apron

1 Put on apron.
2 **Adult:** mix the vegetable or fabric dyes in separate buckets or
containers according to the manufacturer's instructions.
3 Fold the fabric several times to make a small triangle or square.
4 Put on rubber gloves. Dip each corner of the folded fabric into a
different coloured dye. Allow the dyes to meet in the centre of
the fabric. Squeeze out excess dye after each application.
5 Open out the fabric. Hang to dry.

*Gently dip a corner of the fabric into the dye
and allow the excess dye to drip off.*

*Dip the fabric into the second colour so that it
overlaps the edges of the first colour.*

Dyed fabric makes a
terrific cushion cover,
tablecloth or a striking
wall hanging.

reverse dip & dye

you will need

liquid bleach

bucket or large ice-cream
  container

dark-coloured cotton fabric
  (black, dark blue and blue
  denim work well)

rubber gloves

apron

1 Put on apron.
2 **Adult:** pour bleach into the bucket or ice-cream container.
3 Fold the fabric several times to make a small triangle or square.
4 Put on rubber gloves. Dip each corner of the folded fabric into bleach. Hold each corner in the bleach until it changes colour.
5 Open out fabric. Hang to dry.

Safety first

Ensure that bleach does not come in contact with skin. Keep lid on bleach and keep it out of children's reach at all times.

Dip fabric into bleach until the fabric changes colour, then allow excess bleach to drip off.

multi-coloured tie-dyeing

you will need

2 or 3 vegetable dyes or cold-water fabric dyes

2 or 3 buckets or large ice-cream containers

white cotton garment or fabric

rubber bands or string

apron

rubber gloves

1 Put on apron.

2 **Adult:** mix vegetable dyes or cold-water fabric dyes in separate containers according to the manufacturer's instructions.

3 Bunch or roll the fabric and bind it tightly at intervals with rubber bands or string, wrapping over the same spot several times.

4 Put on rubber gloves. Submerge the tied fabric in one dye bucket for a few minutes. Remove fabric and allow excess dye to drip off. Leave fabric until it is semi-dry then remove string and bands. Hang to dry thoroughly.

5 Repeat steps 4 and 5 with the second and third dyes.

Bind fabric tightly and wind string or rubber bands over same spot several times.

Submerge bound fabric in dye bucket for a few minutes then allow excess dye to drip off.

reverse tie-dyeing

you will need

liquid bleach

bucket or ice-cream container

cotton fabric or garment in dark
colour (black, dark blue and
blue denim work well)

string or rubber bands

apron

rubber gloves

1 **Adult:** pour bleach into bucket or ice-cream container.
2 Fold, twist, crumple or roll fabric or garment then bind tightly with
   string or rubber bands wrapping over the same spot several times.
3 Put on apron and rubber gloves. Dip the fabric or garment into
   bleach until the colour of the fabric changes, then allow excess
   bleach to drip off.
4 Rinse fabric or garment thoroughly in cold water until the water is
   no longer coloured. Remove the bands or string. Hang to dry.

Safety first

Ensure that bleach does not come in contact with skin. Keep lid on
bleach and keep it out of reach of children at all times.

*Bind fabric tightly and wind string or rubber
bands over same spot several times.*

*Submerge bound fabric in bleach for a few
minutes until the colour of the fabric changes.*

collage & construction

Collage is an exciting technique of pasting, gluing, taping and stapling materials such as paper, fabrics, dried foods, feathers, nuts and other objects. Encourage tactile exploration and use of objects to create 'feeling' pictures. Construction encourages children to further explore tactile and colour combinations. Working in three dimensions challenges children's imaginations and can present fascinating results. Allow children to work with a wide range of materials including recycled objects, which will enrich both collages and constructions.

paper collage

you will need
coloured paper or tissue paper
glue in tubs
brushes
paper or plastic sheet or lid

1 Tear coloured paper or tissue
paper into different sized pieces.
2 Brush a coloured paper piece
with glue then stick the paper
piece onto the paper, plastic
sheet or lid. Repeat to make a
picture. Younger children
often prefer to add glue directly
to the paper or plastic then
place the paper pieces onto it.
Older children can arrange
their collage materials into
pictures; younger children
will simply enjoy gluing
materials onto the sheet.
For see-through pictures, tissue
paper gives the best result;
the paper pieces overlap,
causing colours to mix and
blend. Tape see-through pictures
to a window for display.

box sculpture

you will need
cardboard boxes, all shapes
 and sizes
cardboard cylinders
powder tempera paint
 (see page 6)
shallow bowl
paintbrush
collage materials
masking tape
heavy wool or string
PVA glue

1 Tape boxes and cylinders together to make space-age cities,
 trains, animals or abstract sculptures.
2 Make up powder tempera paint in shallow bowl. Paint
 cardboard sculpture. Glue on any collage materials.
3 String sculpture together with wool or string. Several small
 structures can be joined together.

note If the sculpture is painted with a clear gloss enamel, the
 writing on the boxes will show through the paint.

box car

Paint and decorate top and sides of upturned box in as many or as few colours as desired.

Using the paper fasteners, attach the metal pie plate headlights to the front of the box.

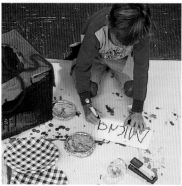

Make a number plate by writing your name on a polystyrene tray, then attach tray to box.

Tie rope to one side of box, place box over child, then adjust length of rope and tie to second side.

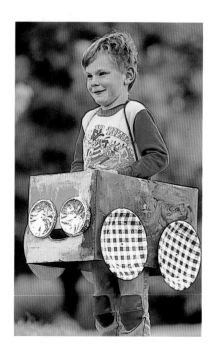

you will need

large cardboard box, top flaps cut off

powder paint in bowls

paintbrushes

4 large paper plates

paper fasteners, about
   2cm (¾in) in length

2 foil pie plates or small paper plates
   covered in foil

felt-tipped pen

small polystyrene packing tray

heavy string or cord

masking tape

stapler

scissors

1 **Adult:** using scissors, cut a hole in bottom of box large enough to slip over child's hips.

2 Turn box upside down. Paint top and sides of box. Allow to dry.

3 **Adult:** using scissors, pierce two holes in each long side of box, where wheels are to be attached. Pierce holes in centre of paper plates. Attach plates to sides of box with paper fasteners. Cover pointed ends of fasteners inside box with tape.

4 Use two foil pie plates as headlights. **Adult:** using scissors, pierce two holes in one short side of box, where headlights are to be attached. Pierce holes in centre of foil plates. Attach plates to box with paper fasteners. Cover pointed ends of fasteners inside box with tape.

5 Using felt-tipped pen, write your name on packing tray to make personalised number plate. Tape or staple to back of box.

6 **Adult:** using scissors, pierce hole in centre of each long side of box, at the top. Thread string or cord through one hole. Tie a double knot so it cannot slip through hole.

7 Step into box and pull it up to the waist. **Adult:** pull string or cord around back of child's neck, then thread through second hole. Tie a double knot to secure string or cord. The car is now ready for a ride.

Make a train by adding more boxes as carriages. Turn boxes upside-down on the ground, one behind the other, and children can climb aboard for a train ride.

OVER
4
YEARS

battleship

you will need

2 x 1 litre (1¾ pint) milk cartons

foil

coloured cardboard cylinder

pen

cotton wool

chenille sticks

adhesive tape

scissors

1 Seal the open end of a milk carton with tape. Cut a piece of foil to fit around entire carton. Carefully cover milk carton with foil lengthways, so that the edges are on the underside of the boat. Tape the edges together.

2 **Adult:** cut off the bottom of the second milk carton about 6cm (2½in) from the base (the ship's upper deck). Turn the carton upside down, and place the cardboard cylinder (about 8cm [3in] high) in the middle of the base. The cylinder is the ship's funnel. Draw around the base of the cylinder with a pen. Pierce inside the circle and cut out a hole. Wrap the carton in foil, carefully folding the foil into the hole. Insert the cylinder into the hole. Decorate chimney with cotton wool for smoke.

3 Tape the chimney and top deck to the ship's body.

4 **Adult:** pierce the top of the ship's body with scissors and insert chenille sticks for aerials. Wrap a chenille stick around the bottom of the chimney.

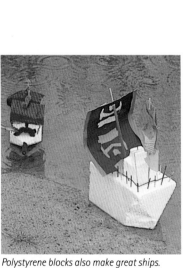

Polystyrene blocks also make great ships. Decorate as desired.

wood collage

you will need
cardboard
wood scraps, all shapes
   and sizes
wood shavings
coloured paper scraps
pencil
PVA glue
scissors

1 Draw an animal, person or
   your house onto cardboard
   (we drew a teddy bear).
   Adult: cut out the shape.
2 Glue a variety of wood scraps
   and shavings onto the shape.
   Leave collage to dry.
3 Cut out features for your
   wood collage from coloured
   paper scraps (we gave our
   bear eyes, nose and a mouth).
   Glue features onto collage.

plaster bandage mask

you will need

plaster bandage
Vaseline
container of water
paint in small bowls
paintbrushes
ribbon or cord
scissors

> Use the mask as a wall decoration when it's not being worn.

1 This activity should be carefully supervised by an adult. Cut the plaster bandage into strips approximately 4cm (1½in) long.

2 **Adult supervision:** tie back the child's hair and generously coat the face with Vaseline so that the mask can be removed easily.

3 Dip a bandage strip in water and place it on child's face. Smooth the bandage strip so that there are no air bubbles or bumps.

4 **Adult supervision:** avoiding the nostrils, mouth and eyes, continue applying the bandage strips, overlapping each bandage strip until the entire face is well covered.

5 Strengthen the mask by adding another layer of plaster bandage. To remove the mask, gently lift the edges to break the suction, then carefully lift the mask from the face. Let the mask dry completely.

6 Trim uneven edges and paint as desired. Make a hole at each side of the face and thread ribbon or cord through to make mask ties.

Dip a bandage strip in water and place it on child's face, then smooth out the strip.

Continue the plastering process but be careful to avoid the child's nostrils, mouth and eyes.

The mask should have a couple of layers of bandage strips to give it added strength.

To remove the mask, gently lift the edges of the mask to break the suction.

Let the mask dry completely, then trim the edges and paint and decorate as desired.

OVER
5
YEARS

fish
kite

you will need

foil liner from orange juice or
   wine cask
small plastic plate
coloured plastic shopping bag
2 plastic cups
paper fasteners or paper clips
felt-tipped pen
string
stapler
adhesive tape
hole puncher
scissors

*Staple the plastic plate rim around the foil
liner opening, at the mouth end of the fish.*

*Staple the intact end of the plastic bag fringe
to the tail end of the fish's body.*

Use the fish as a kite or mobile.

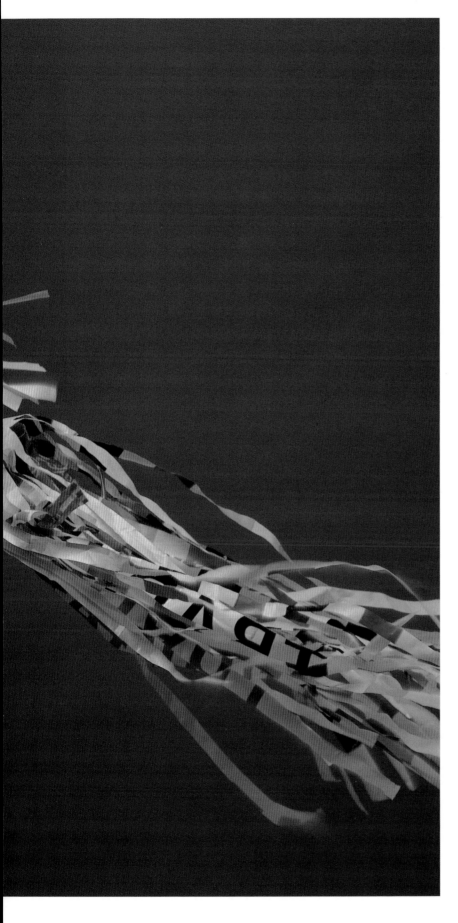

1 **Adult:** cut the ends off the foil liner. Wash out the liner and remove plastic tap. This will be the body of the fish kite. Carefully cut out the centre of the plate leaving the rim intact. Staple the plate rim around the liner opening, at the mouth end. The plate will form the mouth.

2 Fold two or three tucks into the tail end of the liner. Cut the plastic bag into a fringe, leaving the strips of the fringe attached at one end. Staple a large piece of the fringe to the tail end, reserving some fringe for the fins.

3 Staple reserved fringe to fish body.

4 Cut the round base from 2 plastic cups for eyes (or use the remains of the plastic plate). Pierce a hole in the centre of each cup base with scissors and attach eyes to fish using paper fasteners. Draw details with felt-tipped pen.

5 **Adult:** punch a hole through the top of the mouth and thread the string through. Fly the kite.

Tape small pieces of plastic bag fringe to the sides of fish's body for fins.

Decorate the fish's plastic-cup eyes with a black felt-tipped pen.

OVER
3
YEARS

multi-coloured glasses

you will need
egg carton
cellophane pieces
PVA glue or adhesive tape
scissors

1 **Adult:** using scissors make a
large hole in each cup section
of the carton.
2 Glue or tape pieces of coloured
cellophane over each hole. Look
through the cellophane glasses
to see a colourful world.

opera glasses

you will need
foil meal tray
cellophane pieces
iceblock stick
adhesive tape
scissors

1 **Adult:** using scissors, trim
around a foil meal tray and cut
two holes for the lenses.
2 Tape cellophane pieces over
each hole. Tape an iceblock
stick in the centre or at the side
of the glasses, as desired.

binoculars

you will need
cellophane pieces
2 toilet roll cylinders
adhesive tape
string

1 Tape pieces of cellophane over the end
  of the 2 cylinders. Different coloured
  cellophane can be used for each one.
2 Tape the 2 cylinders together.
3 **Adult:** pierce a hole on the outside of
  each cylinder. Attach a string.

telescope

you will need
cellophane scrap
long cardboard cylinder
adhesive tape

1 Tape a piece of cellophane over one end of the cylinder.

weaving & stitching

Fibres, yarns and fabrics provide new tactile experiences, and weaving and sewing help develop the fine motor skills of small hands as well as hand-eye co-ordination. Try not to expect each child's work to exactly replicate the pictures in this book. Treat our projects as a starting point and encourage children to develop their own ideas.

OVER
5
YEARS

nature weaving

you will need
4 sticks about 20cm (8in) long
string
twigs, long grasses, fleece, weeds,
    feathers, flowers and other
    natural objects
scissors

1 Make a square frame by binding the four sticks together
with string at each of the four corners.
2 Wind string firmly around one of the sticks and knot or wrap the
end. Then wind the string onto the stick opposite. Continue winding
string from end to end at regular intervals until the frame is full.
Cut the string and tie end to the frame. These are the warp strings.
3 Starting from one end, weave twigs, grasses, feathers and
other materials under and over the warp strings. Continue until
strings are covered. This weaving makes a beautiful hanging.

*Make a square frame by binding the four
sticks together with string at each corner.*

*Wind string firmly around one of the sticks,
knot the end, then wind it onto opposite stick.*

*Starting from one end, weave the natural
materials under and over the strings.*

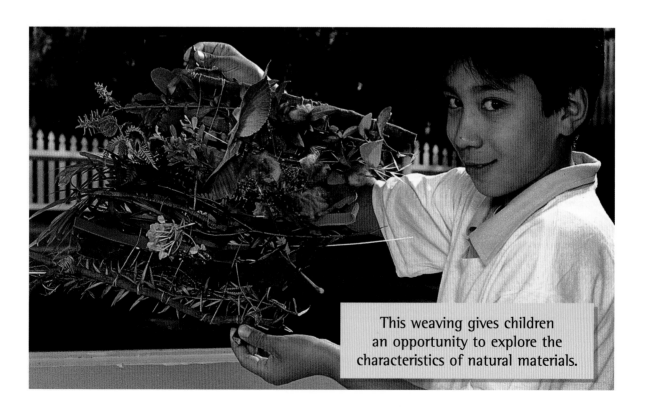

This weaving gives children
an opportunity to explore the
characteristics of natural materials.

branch weaving

you will need

branch with at least 3 smaller
branches shooting out from it
coloured wools, each about
2 metres (2 yards) in length
long grasses, feathers, seashells,
corn husks, seed pods and
other natural objects

1 Starting at the top or bottom
of one small branch, loop wool
around a branch to secure it.
Continue to next small branch
and loop wool around it and
then to the next branch.
Continue to wrap wool around
smaller branches to make a
warp base moving up or down
branches, depending on where
weaving began. Warp threads
are the first threads on the
frame. They are stretched
lengthwise and usually placed
side by side on the frame.

2 Weave wool, grasses and other
intriguingly shaped items
through warp wool strands.
Some children may prefer
to wrap wool around branches
in a random manner.

woven wall hanging

you will need

coloured wool, about 2 metres
(2 yards) in length
U-shaped branch
feathers, leaves, wild grasses,
bamboo, leather strips

1 Tie wool at one end of branch and
stretch to opposite end. Tie off
wool in a knot. Leave about 3cm
(1¼in) between each length of
wool. Repeat stretching wool until
you have filled the available space.

2 Thread through, under and over,
materials such as feathers, leaves,
grasses, bamboo and leather strips.

OVER 8 YEARS

weaving on a box loom

you will need
iceblock sticks
cardboard box
fabric strips or wool
2 dowel rods (at least as wide as the cardboard box)
strip of cord
masking tape
scissors, if needed

1 Tape iceblock sticks, half-way down the stick, at regular intervals along one end of the box. At opposite end of box, tape sticks in line with the first row.

2 Tie a fabric strip or length of wool to the first stick at one end. Take the strip around the first stick at the opposite end, then back again to the next stick on the opposite end. Keep stretching the fabric strip taut. Continue until all sticks are looped. These first strips are the warp threads.

3 Beginning at one end of box, weave fabric strips or wool under and over the warp strips. Continue weaving until warp strips are covered.

4 When weaving is complete, carefully slip the weaving off the sticks and thread the dowel rods through the loops at each end of the weaving. Secure the loose ends by threading these back into the weaving.

5 Attach a hanging cord to the top dowel. Use as a wall hanging.

Tape iceblock sticks, half-way down the stick, at regular intervals along one end of the box.

The warp or first threads are stretched from one end of the box to the other.

The weft threads are woven over and under the warp threads to create the weaving.

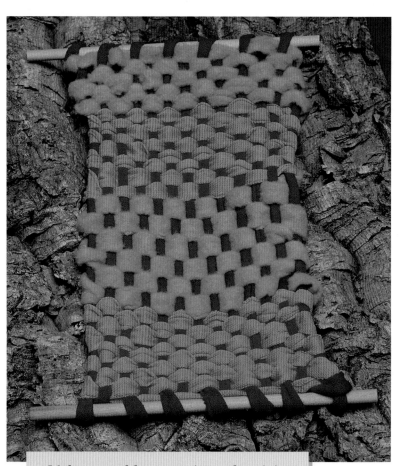

Make several box weavings, then join them together to make a floor mat!

appliquéd placemat

you will need

40cm (16in) x 30cm (12in) piece of
  hessian fabric
felt
pins
wool or sewing thread
blunt or large needle
buttons, braid or lace
scissors

1 Fringe the hessian fabric by removing
   the threads along each edge.
2 Cut out felt shapes to make a design.
   Pin felt pieces onto hessian.
3 Using sewing thread or wool and a
   blunt or large needle, stitch the felt
   pieces to the hessian (for tips on
   using needles, see page 5). First knot
   the thread then bring the needle up
   through the fabric from the wrong
   side. To finish each thread length,
   take the needle through to the back
   of the fabric and make two small
   secure stitches on top of each other.
   Embroidery stitches can be used (see
   diagrams at right).
4 Stitch buttons, braid or lace onto
   the placemat as desired.

*Arrange the different felt pieces into design
before stitching them onto the mat.*

*First knot the thread then bring the needle up
through the fabric from the wrong side.*

Running stitch

Whipped running stitch

Couching

Blanket stitch

weaving & stitching **73**

weaving trays

you will need

polystyrene packing trays

wool threaded through a
  darning needle (see page 5)

ribbon, wool, long reeds or grass
  for weaving

seashells or seed pods

knife

1 **Adult:** cut a geometric section in centre of the tray and remove it; a rectangle is easiest for a beginner to use.

2 Tie knot in end of threaded wool. Put threaded needle through tray, about 3cm (1¼in) in from edge of cut-out shape. Pull the wool across to other side and bring needle up through tray.

3 Repeat this process back and forth across cut-out section to make warp threads. Threads strung in one direction only (eg left to right) tend to make square or rectangular weaves whereas wool strung in all directions across cut-out shape enables unusual circles to be woven.

4 Weave ribbon or double thread of wool back and forth in a straight line or weave one or more circles depending on design of warp strings. To keep weaving square, push needle through side of tray after completing a line then continue weaving. Seashells or seed pods can be strung onto wool during weaving. Long reeds or grasses may also be used in place of ribbon or wool. Younger children need supervision until they have had a little practice. Trays can be used as placemats or wall hangings, or the ends of the warp strings can be cut from the tray, tied together two at a time (to stop weaving from coming undone), to be used as pot holders.

mesh stitching

OVER
4
YEARS

you will need
orange or onion mesh bag
coloured cardboard
colourful yarn
masking tape
scissors

1 **Adult:** cut the bag to give a
   flat piece of mesh fabric. Trim the
   edges of the cardboard to make
   a frame. Cut a piece from the
   inside of the cardboard frame;
   it could be an irregular shape
   such as a heart or a simple star.
2 Tape mesh to the wrong
   side of the cardboard frame.
   Trim excess mesh.
3 Wrap a small piece of tape
   around the end of a yarn
   length (this makes the yarn
   end stiff enough to thread
   through the mesh). Using the
   coloured yarns, stitch patterns
   through the holes in the mesh.

Mesh stitching makes an unusual
wall or window hanging.

Securely tape mesh to the cardboard frame.

Stitch patterns through the holes in the mesh.

tactile play

Sensory awareness goes hand in hand with creativity. Projects in this chapter will stimulate children's imaginations through exploration of texture, temperature and colour, and will arouse their curiosity. Many of these projects are inexpensive, require little preparation and are guaranteed to be fun!

coloured ice melts

you will need

plastic containers of various
   sizes and shapes, suitable for
   freezing, filled with water
food colouring
large plastic containers

1   **Adult with children:** in each of the plastic containers filled with water, add food colouring to water. Freeze the different containers overnight.

2   Look at the patterns formed in the ice by the food colouring; colour will either freeze evenly or coagulate in patches in the ice.

3   Empty coloured ice into a large container of water. Does the ice float or sink? Watch the ice melt; colours will mix, swirl and blend together in the water. Add more food colouring to see the effects. Add dark colours to the bowl last as they will eventually give a dark murky colour to the water.

4   Feel the shapes of the ice. How does the ice feel? Discuss why ice melts.

Do the iceblocks float or sink in the water?

Look at the patterns of colour in the ice.

slime

you will need

1 cup Lux soap flakes
2 litres (3½ pints) warm water
large plastic container
a pinch of food colouring
egg beaters
kitchen gadgets such as a funnel,
   cup, whisk, soup ladle, scoop,
   soap drainers, punnets,
   sponges, jugs, etc

1 **Adult:** dissolve soap flakes in
   warm water in a large
   plastic container. Add food
   colouring. Allow mixture to
   stand until it becomes thick;
   add more water if necessary.
2 **Adult:** beat mixture with egg
   beaters. Children can help too!
3 Use the kitchen gadgets to pour,
   measure, scoop, beat and whisk.
   Children can also use words to
   describe how the mixture feels
   and what they are doing.

*Children enjoy slime but need careful
supervision to avoid soap getting in their eyes.*

mix & mess

you will need

large containers of seeds, dried
   peas, beans, lentils, rice, grains,
   tea, cereal, etc
plastic containers for mixing
spoons, scoops, tongs,
   cup measures

1 **Adult:** arrange containers of
   seeds, etc in the centre of a
   table outdoors or on an easy-
   to-clean area. Give a container
   to each child for mixing.
2 Use scoops, spoons, tongs and
   cup to mix, measure, stir and
   pour, but don't eat!

Gather lots of different seeds, dried peas,
beans, lentils, grains and cereals.

Use scoops, spoons, tongs and cups to mix,
measure, stir and pour the different foods.

Children will enjoy the texture and consistency
of the ingredients and the fun of 'cooking'.

texture rubbings

you will need
textured objects such as fans,
    bark, packaging plastic, combs,
    braid, laces, fabric, coins
sheet of paper
crayons

1 **Adult:** flimsy materials such
   as braid and lace can be glued,
   pinned or taped onto a board
   to keep them rigid.
2 Select a few textured objects.
   Place paper over the textured
   surfaces. Rub paper with crayon.
3 Try mixing crayon colours and
   using several textured surfaces
   on the one sheet of paper.

   Older children might like to make
   a texture rubbing as above but
   use white candles instead of
   crayons. Then paint over the paper
   with a thin water-based paint.

For this texture rubbing, we used a fan
which was woven out of cane.

Use white candles instead of crayons and
then paint over the paper with thin paint.

tactile play 81

ALL
AGES

clay wind chime

you will need

clay (see page 6)
tools such as nails, biscuit
    cutters, garlic press, knives
spatula
fishing line
coat-hanger or branch
rolling pin
ceramic kiln

1 **Adult:** knead a small portion of
  clay to ensure that there are no
  air bubbles in it. (Clay with air
  bubbles in it will explode when it
  is fired in a kiln.) Roll out the clay
  to 1cm (3/8in) to 2cm (3/4in) thick.

2 Cut desired shape out of flat clay.
  Using the tools, gently press
  texture marks into clay shape
  and attach additional pieces
  of clay. Make a hole in the top
  and bottom of each piece for
  hanging. Slide spatula under
  shape and move it to a place
  to dry. Make a dozen or more
  different shapes for wind chimes.

3 **Adult:** when thoroughly dry take
  the shapes to a school or craft
  shop kiln to be bisque fired. This
  gives them the ringing quality of
  wind chimes.

4 **Adult:** tie short pieces of fishing
  line through the holes in the
  chimes. About four knots need to
  be made in fishing line to keep
  items in place. Tie three or four
  chimes together in a row to make
  a string of chimes. Tie strings
  of chimes to a branch or coat-
  hanger. The fishing line gives the
  chimes a better tone, but wool
  may be used.

play dough creatures

you will need
different coloured play dough
  (see page 9)
plastic eyes or buttons
chenille sticks

1 Mould colourful dough into unusual creatures. Roll or pound play dough
  into fat round shapes, long thin sausage shapes or odd geometric shapes.
2 Add different coloured play dough or stick-on plastic eyes, buttons or
  chenille sticks to make interesting features. There's no end to the fantastic
  creations a child's imagination can produce from supple play dough.

puppets

Few crafts come to life as delightfully as handcrafted puppets. They encourage self-expression, promote interaction with play partners and help to develop social and communication skills. Some children can communicate more easily through their puppet character in a pretend world. The puppets in these projects are made by techniques ranging from papier-mâché to simple sewing. Larger puppets are best tackled by a group of children. A good follow-up activity is to devise and perform a puppet play.

glove puppet

you will need
fabric, felt and fur scraps,
    wool, buttons, beads or
    feathers, as desired
PVA glue or needle and thread
plain, long or short glove
fabric crayon
scissors

1 Ask children about the type of
    glove puppet they would like
    to make. Animal pictures may
    provide inspiration and ideas;
    our puppet was created from a
    picture of a panda. Imaginary
    creatures can also be created.
2 Glue or stitch felt, wool, fur or
    buttons onto the glove to create
    the puppet you desire.

    Children might like to create a
    group of animals and have a
    different creature on each finger.

All you need is an old glove, fabric scraps, a
needle and thread, and a little imagination.

sock puppet

you will need
sock
thin black cardboard
PVA glue
felt
buttons
needle and thread
scissors

1 Cut a slit in the sock, from the small toe area to the large toe area.
2 Cut a cardboard rectangle about 7cm (2¾in) x 20cm (8in) and curve the corners. (The rectangle should be able to fit into the sock.)
3 Fold the cardboard rectangle in half to form the inside of the mouth. Place the cardboard inside the slit of the sock, aligning the rounded edge with sock edge. Glue in place.
4 Decorate your puppet to create an animal or fantasy creature by stitching on felt shapes for body features such as tongue, ears or nose, and sew on buttons for eyes.

Place the folded cardboard rectangle in the slit of the sock, aligning the rounded edge with the sock edge. Glue the cardboard in place.

easy sock puppet

you will need
sock
PVA glue or fabric glue or darning needles threaded with wool (children over five years may be able to use large sewing needles)
felt, ribbon, wool and fabric scraps
buttons
feathers, sequins

1 Put hand inside sock to prevent sewing or gluing both sides of the sock together.
2 Glue or sew on any of the materials to create an animal or person out of the sock. Plastic eyes or buttons are excellent for eyes.

hamburger puppet

you will need

takeaway hamburger pack

4 strong large rubber bands

pair of coloured tights

2 plastic teaspoons

foil packet

2 paper ring reinforcements
(coloured with a felt-tipped
pen) or stickers

plastic bread-wrapper tie

felt-tipped pen

cardboard milk carton

adhesive tape

scissors

Safety first

Keep plastic bread-wrapper
ties out of the reach of small
children as these ties are
extemely dangerous if swallowed.

1 Open the hamburger pack and place two strong rubber bands over each side of the hamburger pack, near the hinge. The puppet's mouth will open and close when fingers and thumb are placed through each band from behind the hinge of the pack.

2 Pull tights over the hamburger pack, from behind the hinge, placing waist inside the pack. Pull a strong rubber band over the tights and across the hinge of the hamburger pack. Legs should hang at each side of the hinge. Cut the tights behind the hinge to make an opening for your hand.

3 **Adult:** make slits at top and front edge of hamburger pack and push teaspoon handles through from top to front edge to make eyes and tusks.

4 Cut the foil packet in a fringe leaving strip attached at one end.

5 Roll up the foil packet and tape in a roll at the intact end.
Adult: make a small slit in the back of the hamburger pack and push the taped end of the packet through the slit to make the puppet's hair.

6 Place stickers on spoons for eyes or draw with a felt-tipped pen. A bread tie hooked around tights at the front edge, between the puppet's tusks, makes the nose. Draw nostrils on the bread tie with a felt-tipped pen.

7 The legs of the tights make the puppet's legs. Tie knots halfway down the legs to make knees. Cut out some feet from the milk carton. Draw claws on feet with a felt-tipped pen. **Adult:** make a small slit in each foot and push the tights through. Knot the tights under each foot to secure them.

The hamburger puppet can be made from lots of recycled materials found around the house.

Pull two strong rubber bands over the whole of the hamburger pack, near the hinge.

Pull tights over the hamburger pack, from behind the hinge, placing waist inside pack.

Make slits at top and front edge of the pack and push teaspoon handles from top to front.

Roll up foil fringe and tape intact end, then slip it into slit at back of hamburger pack.

Make slits in the milk-carton feet and push legs through slit, then tie a knot under feet.

finger puppets

you will need
felt, about 9cm (3½in) x 8cm (3¼in)
sewing machine
fabric scraps, buttons,
  sequins, feathers
PVA or fabric glue
scissors

1 **Adult:** cut two pieces of felt, about
  6cm (2½in) long and 4cm (1½in) wide.
2 **Adult:** place one piece of felt on top of
  the other. Sew a zigzag stitch around the
  felt, making the top rounded and leaving
  the bottom open for finger access.
3 Glue or sew on any fabric scraps, buttons,
  or sequins to create an animal or person.

paper finger puppets

you will need
felt-tipped pens
coloured cardboard
collage materials
PVA glue
adhesive tape
scissors

1 Draw a face or animal shape onto the cardboard, about
  8cm (3¼in) long and 5cm (2in) wide. **Adult:** cut out shape.
2 **Adult:** cut a rectangular strip of cardboard long enough to
  wind around the child's finger, leaving space for glue or tape.
3 Glue or tape ends of strip together to make a circle.
4 Glue back of cut-out drawing onto cardboard circle.
5 Decorate puppet with paper, feathers or other collage materials.

stick figure puppets

you will need
children's drawings
cardboard
iceblock sticks
PVA glue
adhesive tape
scissors

1 Glue drawings onto cardboard. Drawing around a hand makes an interesting shape for a child to make into a creature.
2 **Adult:** cut out drawing. Tape iceblock stick to the back of the cardboard. This becomes the handle with which to hold and play-act with the puppet.

wooden spoons

you will need
wooden spoons
powder paint mixed in small bowl
paintbrushes
wool or cotton wool
felt-tipped pens
fabric scraps
PVA glue

1 Paint wooden spoon white or light colour.
2 Glue wool strands or cotton wool onto spoon for hair. If using wool strands it is easier to glue wool around the edge of spoon across the top and then add another layer running from front to back.
3 Paint or draw face onto spoon. Inside and outside surfaces are both suitable.
4 Wrap fabric around handle. Secure with glue.

Crepe paper, tissue paper or foil can also be used to cover the handle.

spider

you will need

soft drink bottle base
red fabric scrap
thread
ballpoint pen
stickers for eyes
felt-tipped pen
stapler
scissors

1 Cut off a strip from around the rim of the bottle base.
2 Cut the strip into eight thin legs.
3 **Adult:** soften the remaining base piece in hot water. Push out the bottom of the base to make it rounded.
4 **Adult:** staple the legs around the edge of the base, positioning them so that they curve out from the body.
5 Cut the fabric scrap into strips and tie in a bundle with thread. Punch two holes in the base with a ballpoint pen. Insert a length of thread through the holes. Tie the bundle of fabric strips over the holes to make hair.
6 Add stickers for eyes. Draw details with felt-tipped pen.

Cut a strip from around the rim of bottle base.

Cut the bottle base strip into eight thin legs.

Push softened base out so that it's rounded.

Staple the legs around base so they curve out.

Tie bundle of strips over the holes to make hair.

cuppa snake

you will need

ballpoint pen
30 coloured plastic cups
pantihose leg or a stocking
newspaper
2 coloured plastic plates
felt-tipped pen
paper fasteners or stapler
fishing line, if desired
stick, if desired
scissors

1 Using a ballpoint pen, punch a hole in the base of each cup. Thread cups onto the pantihose leg through the hole in the cup base. To space cups apart, place a ball of newspaper into each cup after it is threaded.

2 For the head, cut the rim off a plastic plate and punch two holes in eye positions with a ballpoint pen. Punch a large third hole at the edge of the plate, above and between the eyes and thread the end of the pantihose through this hole. Thread the pantihose end through the base of another cup which will be a hat. Secure head and hat by tying a knot in pantihose.

3 Cut the base off two plastic cups to make eyes. Draw on the eyes with a felt-tipped pen. Attach each base to plate with paper fasteners or stapler. Cut a strip from second plastic plate shaped like a tongue. Punch a hole and attach tongue underneath head using a paper fastener.

4 Cut a triangular plastic piece from the plate for the tail tip. Punch a hole through the wide end of the plastic piece and thread it onto the end of the snake's tail. Knot the pantihose at the tail end to secure the tail.

To make a moving snake, punch holes at three points along the snake. Attach a piece of fishing line at each point, and tie the other end of each piece to the stick. Shake the stick and the snake will wriggle.

Cuppa snake is made from recycled materials.

Space cups apart with balls of newspaper.

Thread pantihose through final cup for a hat.

cylinder puppet

you will need

fabric pencil or pen
felt, pink and contrasting colours
long cardboard cylinder
cardboard scraps
fabric scraps
wool or raffia
buttons
PVA glue
scissors

1 Using a child's hand as a guide, draw a three-fingered hand shape onto the felt. Cut out the felt making the piece at least 3cm (1¼in) larger than the child's hand.

2 Cut the cardboard cylinder into three pieces; one 7cm (2¾in) long and two 5cm (2in) long. Glue the two short pieces to the outer finger and thumb sections of the felt hand; these will make the puppet's hands. Glue the centre finger section inside the 7cm-long cylinder to make the puppet's head.

3 Cover the head cylinder with pink felt. Glue on a rolled felt strip for the puppet's nose. Cut out two hand shapes from pink felt and glue them inside the hand cylinder.

4 Cut legs and shoes from cardboard and cover in fabric or felt. Glue onto main felt piece.

5 Cut clothes from fabric scraps and wool. Use felt scraps and buttons for facial features. Make hair from wool or raffia and glue onto the head cylinder. The girl puppet's hair was made by taking a bundle of yarns and plaiting at each end, leaving an unplaited section in the centre. The boy's hair is raffia.

Make cylinder puppets based on characters from a favourite storybook and use the puppets to tell the story.

Use contrasing colours for felt and brightly coloured fabric scraps to dress up the puppets.

Glue the two short cyclinders onto back of arms and the long cylinder into the head.

Cover head cylinder with pink felt and cut out pink hands and glue into short cylinders.

white poodle

you will need

15 or more thin white plastic
   shopping bags
rectangular polystyrene piece
old ballpoint pen
thick white sock
4 rubber bands
black or pink felt-tipped pen
newspaper
2 plastic teaspoons
pink fabric scrap (for tongue)
stiff black plastic, such as a soft
   drink bottle base
star stickers
2 pairs of white pantihose
   or stockings
4 plastic lids, such as those from
   margarine containers
fishing Line
PVA glue
adhesive tape
scissors

The white poodle can be made out of lots of different materials recycled from home.

1 Cut the bottom seam and handles off each shopping bag. Cut the sides of the bag so that you have two pieces. To make the poodle's body, place the polystyrene piece on a flat surface and push the plastic bags into the polystyrene using the flat end of a ballpoint pen. Continue until one side of the polystyrene is well covered. This will be the top side of the poodle.

2 Trim the plastic bag ends so that the coat is approximately the same length all over, but long enough to cover the edges of the polystyrene.

3 Make a nose at the toe of the sock by holding a couple of tucks with a rubber band. Colour the nose black or pink with a felt-tipped pen.

4 Stuff the foot of the sock firmly with balls of newspaper. Make the poodle's topknot by putting a rubber band around the heel of the sock. Stuff more newspaper into the leg of the sock.

5 Draw eyes on plastic teaspoons with a felt-tipped pen. Slip the spoon handles under the rubber band that holds the topknot. Cut a long strip of a plastic bag to make ears. Slip the centre of the plastic strip over the topknot and under the rubber band around the topknot.

6 Cut a strip of pink fabric and slip it under the rubber band at the nose. Trim the tongue to the right length and shape then secure with glue.

7 Place a rubber band over each end of the polystyrene body piece. Loop the neck end of the sock onto the band at one end of the body. Tie a fringed plastic bag around base of neck to hide where it joins the body.

8 Cut a thick strip of black plastic for the collar. Decorate with star stickers and put around the poodle's neck. Secure with tape if necessary.

9 Cut the legs off the pantihose. Tie the pantihose legs through the rubber bands at both ends of the poodle's body so that a leg hangs down on each corner of the body. Cut feet off pantihose.

10 Push a plastic lid inside each leg and knot the pantihose leg under each lid. To hold the lid in place, gather the pantihose above the lid and wrap tape around pantihose.

11 Tie a length of fishing line to the top of head and to rubber band at tail end of body. Hold fishing line to make the poodle walk, sit or stand.

Lay the polystyrene on a flat surface and push plastic pieces into polystyrene using a pen.

Make the nose by gathering a couple of tucks with a rubber band and colour it black or pink.

The plastic piece for the ears and the spoon eyes slip under the band around the topknot.

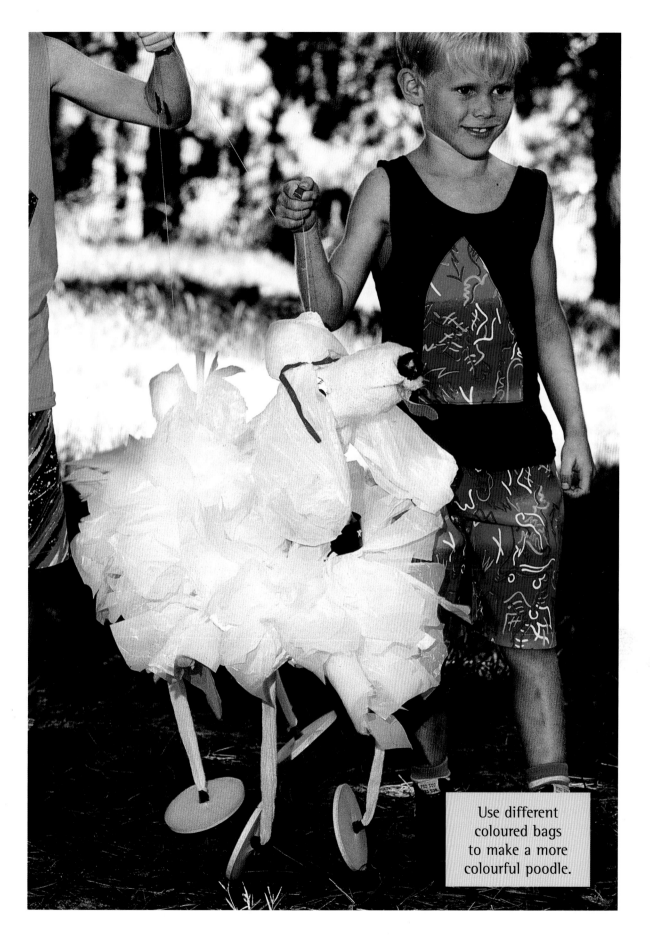

Use different
coloured bags
to make a more
colourful poodle.

broom puppet

you will need

broom or mop

dowel rod about 60cm (24in)

felt-tipped pens

cardboard

buttons, fringe, chenille sticks
   (for facial features)

old long-sleeve men's shirt

2 pieces of cord or string, about
   50cm (20in) long

2 dowel rods about 90cm (36in)

masking tape

PVA glue

stapler

scissors

1   Stand the broom or mop bristle-end up. Tape the small dowel
     across the broom handle below the bristle end to make a t-shape.
     This will form the shoulders of the puppet.

2   Draw a large face shape on cardboard. Cut out the face shape.
     Tape the face shape to the broom handle so that the bristles or
     mop top stick out above the face like hair.

3   Glue on a cardboard shape for nose. Add button eyes, fringing for
     eyebrows, chenille sticks for ears and draw facial features as desired.

4   Dress puppet in the shirt. Cut two hands from cardboard. Staple a hand
     and a piece of cord (at about halfway down the cord) to each sleeve cuff.

5   Tie the cord to one of the remaining dowel rods. Repeat for other hand.
     Two children can move the puppet, one operating the arm-control rods;
     however it's easier with three children, one on each rod.

*Tape the small dowel across the broom handle
below the bristle end to make a t-shape.*

*Tape the face shape to the broom handle so
that the bristles or mop top stick out like hair.*

*Glue a cardboard nose shape onto the face
and add puppet facial features as desired.*

*Staple a cardboard hand shape to sleeve cuff
then staple the cord to the sleeve cuff.*

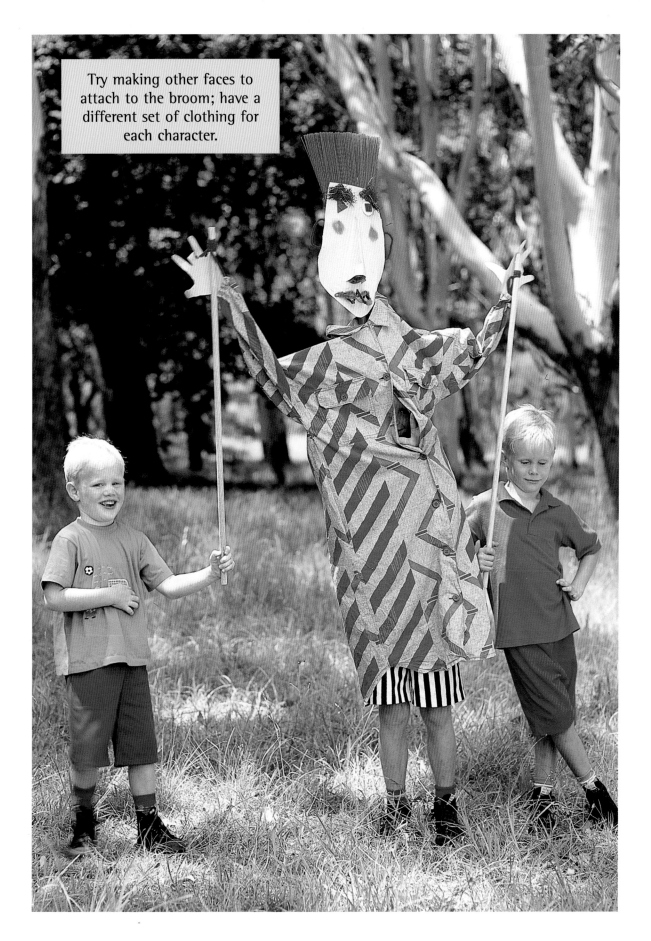

Try making other faces to attach to the broom; have a different set of clothing for each character.

monster puppet

you will need

large foam block or small pieces
  glued together (for head)
thin foam piece (for teeth)
iceblock sticks
paint in small bowls
paintbrushes
50cm (20in) red felt or fabric
  piece (for tongue)
3 metres (3 yards) of 115cm-wide
  (45in) calico (for body)
fabric strips, yarn, fringing
3 hoops (cane or plastic) or
  6 metres (20ft) garden hose
1.5 metres (1½ yards) cotton tape
thick wool and darning needle,
  if desired
PVA glue
Stanley knife or electric knife
scissors

1. **Adult:** using scissors, Stanley knife or electric knife, carve a head shape from the foam block. Cut chunks from the block to give it a lumpy texture.

2. **Adult:** carve a hollow to fit the child's head in the under section of the monster head. Glue or tie another piece of foam to form the mouth or cut an opening in the large block. (We tied cotton tape around the head and folded a thin rectangular piece of foam over the tape.)

3. Cut a zigzag pattern from a thin foam piece to make teeth. Glue this piece to the inside of the mouth. Glue on foam pieces for eyes. Add iceblock sticks for eyelashes. (Ping pong balls could be used for eyeballs, if desired.)

4. Paint the monster's head in suitable colours. Tie or glue the felt or fabric piece inside the mouth. Cut into shape for tongue.

5. Decorate the body by making small cuts in the calico and tying fabric strips or fringing through the cuts. Fabric strips can be plaited, have buttons tied on, or just left hanging. The body could also be painted.

6. **Adult:** cut hoops in half; or if using garden hose, cut six 1 metre (39in) lengths and bend into a semi-circle.

7. Cut the cotton tape into six equal lengths. Position hoop or hose pieces at regular intervals under the body fabric. Make slits in the fabric and thread the cotton tape through the slits to secure the hoop pieces to the fabric. The hoops shape the body and provide handholds for operators.

8. Tie, glue or stitch body fabric to the back of the head. Tie or stitch fringing at the back of the head for the mane or attach extra fabric strips or yarn. To operate the monster puppet, each child holds a hoop and one child stands underneath the head.

To make a dragon, add a strip of zigzag spine down the puppet's back and decorate the body fabric with fabric cut into the shape of scales.

We attached the mouth by tying cotton tape around the head and folding a thin rectangular piece of foam over the tape.

Tie or glue the felt or fabric piece inside the mouth, then cut a shape in the tongue. We cut ours into a three-pronged tongue.

Position hoop or hose pieces at regular intervals under fabric, then thread cotton tape through slits and tie around hoop to secure.

The monster can be used at parades, festivals, school fetes and plays.

celebrations

Celebrations are exciting and joyous times for children and they'll adore being involved in the preparations. Piñatas, party masks, musical instruments and sweet treats are sure to make that birthday party extra special. Bunnies, bonnets and decorated eggs make great projects for Easter, while Christmas trimmings and decorations encourage children to explore creativity in Christmas themes.

musical instruments

rhythm sticks

you will need
paint in small bowls
paintbrushes
2 dowel rods about 30cm (12in) long and
   1cm (³⁄₈in) to 2cm (³⁄₄in) thick
clear gloss enamel

1 Paint dowel rods. Leave to dry.
2 **Adult:** coat sticks with clear gloss enamel.
   Hit sticks in time to music.

*The photograph below shows children with, from back, rhythm sticks,
balloon shaker, tambourine, string instrument, bell and paper shakers.*

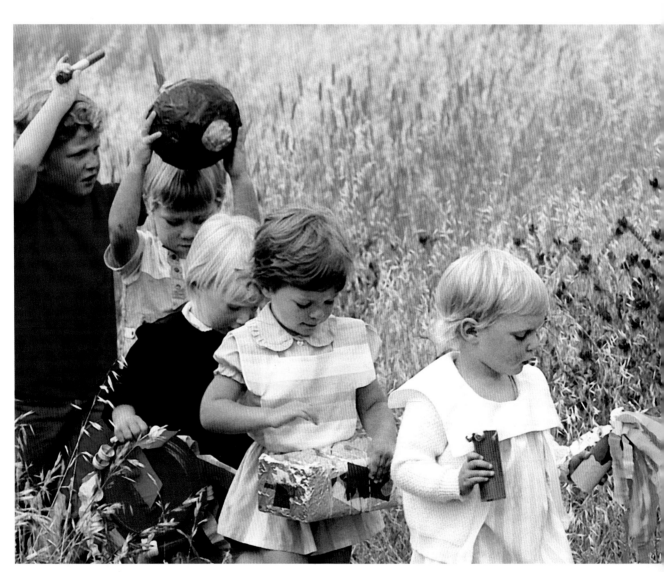

string instrument

you will need

heavy small box without lid
   (shoe box is a good size)
paint in small bowls
paintbrushes
collage materials
rubber bands of different thicknesses
   and widths

1 Decorate box with paint and collage materials.
   Allow to dry.
2 Put rubber bands around box. To play, strum
   the rubber bands.

---

tambourine

you will need

2 plastic plates or 3 uncoated paper plates
paint in small bowls
paintbrushes
wool
metal bottle caps with a hole punched in them
   (or seashells or similar noisy items)
crepe paper or coloured tissue paper streamers
PVA glue
hole puncher
tape or stapler

1 Glue plates together for added strength.
   Paint paper plates.
2 **Adult:** punch holes around rim of plate,
   about 5cm (2in) apart.
3 Thread wool through holes around plate,
   adding two bottle caps at a time in five or
   six places.
4 **Adult:** tie the ends of the wool together
   in a knot.
5 Tape or staple crepe paper or tissue streamers
   around wool.

balloon shaker

you will need

papier-mâché balloon (see page 107)
½ cup of dried beans, corn, rice or sand
powder paint mixed in small bowls (powder paint
   covers newsprint well)
paintbrushes
clear gloss enamel
masking tape
scissors

1 **Adult:** cut a small hole in the papier-mâché balloon
   and puncture the balloon.
2 Put in beans, corn, rice or sand. Put at least four
   layers of masking tape over the hole.
3 Paint shaker with white paint (to prevent newsprint
   showing through) and allow to dry. Paint with bright
   colours and allow to dry.
4 **Adult:** coat balloon shaker with clear gloss enamel
   to stop the paint rubbing off.

---

bell shaker

you will need

cardboard cylinder, about 15cm (6in) long
tissue paper
liquid starch
wool
metal jingle bells
hole puncher

1 **Adult:** punch holes 1cm (³/₈in) apart around one
   end of cylinder.
2 Decorate cylinder with tissue paper applied with
   liquid starch. Allow to dry.
3 Thread the wool through holes in the cylinder and
   adding a bell between each wool loop.
4 **Adult:** tie ends of wool in a knot.

For variation, glue or staple foil or paper streamers
to one end of cylinder to make a paper shaker.

paper bag piñata

Real piñatas, made from pottery and originating in Mexico, are centrepieces at celebrations. They are filled with sweets, tiny presents, flowers and other treasures. When hit with a stick, piñatas explode into fragments and shower their contents into the uplifted hands of party guests. For children, piñatas are made to be broken more easily, as on this page, with the simple paper bag example. More sturdy piñatas, using papier-mâché techniques, are on the right.

you will need

newspaper
paper bags
string, about 1 metre (1 yard)
   in length
powder paint mixed in small bowls
   (powder paint covers newsprint)
paintbrushes
tissue paper
paper paste or liquid starch
crepe paper
sweets
blindfold
stick, about 1 metre (39in) in length
   and 3cm (1¼in) thick
scissors

1 Scrunch up the newspaper. Fill paper bag with the newspaper to make the bag firm so it is easier to paint. Tie the end of the paper bag with string.

2 Cover paper bag with paint and/or tissue paper applied with paste or liquid starch. If desired, take crepe paper and fold several times to form a 5cm (2in) strip. On one fold make repeated 3cm (1¼in) cuts close together. Run fingers across loops to separate them a little. With loops pointing up, glue uncut side around bag. Allow to dry.

3 Untie end of bag and remove newspaper. Fill bag with sweets; retie string.

4 **Adult:** tie bag to ceiling with string, keeping bag well down from ceiling so as not to cause any damage with stick. Child wearing a blindfold stands near piñata and swings at it with stick, trying to break it open. After four or five attempts, the blindfold and stick should be given to another child to try and break piñata. When piñata breaks open, sweets will fall out for children to collect. All spectators should stand well clear of the child with the stick! At a party, it is a good idea to have one piñata for every four children so that each child gets a turn at trying to break it.

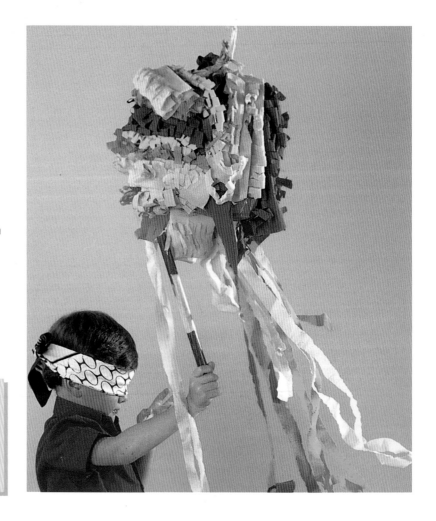

The paper bag piñata is very simple to make. Other good party ideas: face painting, dressing up and treasure hunts.

papier-mâché fish piñata

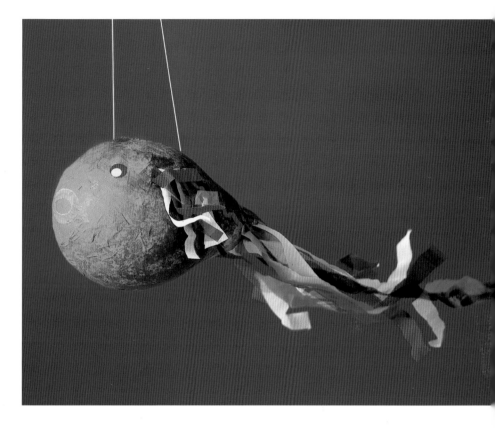

OVER 3 YEARS

you will need
balloon
coloured newsprint or newspaper
paper paste (see page 5)
powder paint mixed in
   small bowls
paintbrushes
strips of crepe and
   cellophane paper
collage materials
masking tape
sweets
scissors

1 **See steps 1 and 2 below.**
3 Paint piñata with bright colours,
   to make fish, bird, animal or
   abstract creation. Tape on
   crepe streamers and collage
   materials for decoration. Leave
   piñata to dry.
4 **Adult:** cut a small lid in the top,
   prick balloon and pull it out. Fill
   hollow with sweets. Tape hole up.

papier-mâché balloon

you will need
balloon
newspaper
paper paste (see page 5)
powder paint mixed in small
   bowls (powder paint covers
   newsprint well)
paintbrushes
lacquer or clear gloss enamel

1 Blow up balloon and tie a double knot
   in the end.
2 Tear newspaper into strips. Place a strip
   into paper paste and cover completely
   with paste. Take strip from paste and wrap
   it around balloon. Repeat process until
   balloon has about three layers of paper
   around it. Allow to dry thoroughly (it takes
   one or two days, depending on the layers
   of newspaper).
3 Paint a colourful design on the balloon.
   Allow to dry thoroughly.
4 **Adult:** coat papier-mâché balloon with
   lacquer or clear gloss enamel.

*Dip newspaper strip in paste so strip is
completely covered, then cover balloon with
strip. Repeat until balloon has three layers.*

treats to eat

rice bubble creatures

you will need

50g butter or margarine
250g marshmallows
2–3 cups of Rice Bubbles
currants, glacé cherries, licorice,
    peppermints, candied
    citrus pieces
chenille sticks
frying pan
spoon
foil

1 **Adult:** melt butter/margarine in frying pan on low heat. Add marshmallows and continue stirring until marshmallows are melted, or microwave together on high for 2 minutes
2 **Adult:** while stirring, add enough Rice Bubbles to make a stiff consistency (approximately 2–3 cups). Remove from heat.
3 Tear off large pieces of foil (about 30cm (12in)) for each child. Lightly grease foil.
4 Put a little butter on inside of hands. While mixture is just warm (not hot), mould into desired shape. Decorate as desired with dried fruit and chenille sticks.

sweet insects

you will need

sweets, such as freckles, licorice all-sorts,
    candy-coated chocolates, candy bananas
clear plastic wrap
coloured chenille sticks

1 Place sweets on strips of plastic wrap and wind the wrap around them to form shapes.
2 Twist chenille sticks at appropriate intervals to form head, bodies and legs. These quaint creatures are great for birthday party table decorations or for hanging with other baubles on the Christmas tree.

bonnets

you will need

children's paintings
collage materials
silk or plastic flowers
crepe paper or coloured wool
PVA glue
stapler
scissors

A
cut
about 35cm or 14in

B
cut
about 40cm or 16in

C
about 60cm or 24in

C

C

1 Select one of the bonnet patterns shown below left. **Adult:** trace the pattern onto an old painting. Cut bonnet out.

2 Glue collage materials and flowers onto bonnet. Allow to dry.

3 **Adult:** glue or staple crepe paper or wool to each side of bonnet to act as an under-chin tie. For variation, cover bonnet shapes with foil, tissue paper or cellophane before decorating.

Hat A Roll paper into a cone and staple at bottom. Staple a ribbon or crepe paper streamer on each side of bonnet to act as a tie.

Hat B Make a cut from edge of circle to centre. Overlap two pieces by about 8cm (3in) to form a slight peak, similar to a Chinese-style hat. Staple together. Staple ribbons to inside of bonnet.

Hat C Place the cut-out shape around the child's head to get the correct size. Staple the ends of the bonnet together.

note It's easier to decorate bonnets before they are stapled together.

batik eggs

you will need

fresh raw eggs, or whole hard-
  boiled eggs

pin

crepe paper (assorted colours)

hot water

1 tablespoon of white vinegar

candle

matches

spoon

bowl

scissors

We 'blew' raw eggs by making a small hole with a pin in both ends of egg and blowing out the contents (it takes a bit of puff!). This way the yolks and whites can be used in cooking. However, the blown egg is quite fragile and if you prefer, hard-boiled eggs can be used. They should keep indefinitely, as the contents of eggs will dry up without odour, unless the shell cracks.

1 To make the dye, cut strips of crepe paper about 2cm (¾in) wide and place in a bowl. **Adult:** cover with hot water to release the dye.

2 Remove crepe paper from dye with a spoon. Add white vinegar to set dye. Allow dye to cool.

3 **Adult:** the eggs are decorated with several applications of wax and dye. Start with the lightest colour and work to the darkest. If you wish to leave any sections of the eggshell surface its natural colour, drip candle wax onto that area. Dip the egg in the lightest dye (yellow, perhaps). It may take a few minutes to reach the desired colour. Dry with a tissue. **Adult:** drip wax onto the sections you want to keep yellow. Dip egg in the darker dye, until it is the desired colour and dry with a tissue. Repeat the process until you have used all the desired colours.

4 **Adult:** to remove wax, place egg on a tray in a moderate oven. When wax has melted (about 2 minutes), wipe dry with a tissue.

For variation, make leaf-printed eggs. Take a small piece of fern or ivy and hold it onto the egg. Secure the leaf in place by wrapping a piece of stocking very firmly around the egg. Tie top of stocking with elastic band and dip egg in dye. Remove excess dye with a tissue and, when dry, peel off stocking and leaves to reveal pattern.

Safety first
Adult supervision is necessary as hot water and hot wax are used.

Place strips of crepe paper in a bowl and pour hot water over strips to release the dye.

Leave some of the egg's natural colour by dripping wax on the egg before dipping in dye.

Dip the egg in the yellow dye or if using a shallow dish, spoon the dye over the egg.

Carefully drip the candle wax onto the sections that you want to keep yellow.

With a spoon, dip the egg into the second dye and leave in dye until egg is desired colour.

For the leaf-printed egg, wrap a leaf around the egg and secure leaf with a tight-fitting stocking.

ALL AGES

tree decorations

pasta ornaments

you will need
pencil
cardboard
coloured and uncoloured
  pasta shapes (see page 6)
gold or silver spray
  paint, if desired
newspaper, if desired
ribbon
PVA glue
hole puncher
scissors

1 Draw Christmas shapes onto
   the cardboard.
2 **Adult:** cut out shapes. Glue
   several identical shapes together
   for added strength. Punch or
   make hole in one end of shape.
3 Glue pasta onto one side. If
   desired, pasta can be glued onto
   other side. Other appropriate
   collage materials may be used.
   Allow glue to dry.
4 **Adult:** if desired, spray
   ornaments with gold or
   silver paint. Spread newspaper
   in well-ventilated area. Lay
   ornament on newspaper, spray
   with paint and allow to dry.
5 Thread ribbon through hole and
   hang ornament on tree.

metal pie plates

you will need
pencil or paintbrush
small foil pie plates
glitter
string or ribbon
PVA glue

1 **Adult:** punch a hole into pie
   plate with a pencil or the
   end of a paintbrush.
2 Apply glue to pie plates (either
   side for different effects). Apply
   glitter to glued areas. Shake off
   excess glitter. Allow to dry.
3 Thread ribbon through hole and
   tie ornament to tree.

For variation, a pattern of holes
could be made and threaded with
coloured wool or ribbon. Strips of
cellophane could also be glued.

egg cup bells

you will need
egg carton
foil
glitter
collage materials
coloured chenille sticks
clear craft glue
scissors

1 **Adult:** cut egg carton into cups.
2 Cut a circle from foil about 15cm
   (6in) in diameter. Place egg cup
   in centre of foil circle and wrap
   foil around it loosely so that
   irregularities in its shape are not
   too noticeable. Press gently.
3 Apply glue to foil and sprinkle
   with glitter. Other collage
   materials may be glued on but
   paint cannot be successfully
   applied to foil that is very
   wrinkled or lumpy.
4 **Adult:** pierce hole in top of bell
   with scissors or other sharply
   pointed instrument.
5 Place a chenille stick through the
   hole in each
   bell and bend
   the end inside
   so bell will
   not slip off. A
   jingle bell can
   be attached to
   chenille stick
   inside. Bend a
   hook shape into
   other end and
   hang the bell
   on branch of
   Christmas tree.

hairpin ornaments

you will need

thick paper or cardboard
hairpins
ribbon, about 20cm (8in) long
newspaper
silver or gold spray paint
PVA glue
scissors

1 **Adult:** cut two circles of paper about 3cm (1¼in) in diameter. Put glue in centre of circle and place about eight hairpins onto glue, leaving rounded edges of hairpins touching in centre.
2 Loop ribbon so both ends are touching, then glue ribbon to other paper circle. When glue and hairpins are almost set, place other circle of paper on top of pins, ribbon-side down. Press firmly. Allow ornament to dry.
3 **Adult:** spread newspaper in well-ventilated area. Lay ornament on newspaper and spray with gold or silver paint. Allow to dry. Tie ornament to Christmas tree.

For variation, paint hairpins with glue and roll them in glitter. Make other decorative shapes.

note Children under four years may need help to arrange hairpins.

polystyrene trays

you will need

polystyrene tray
thick powder paint mixed with dishwashing liquid in small bowls (see page 6)
paintbrushes
tissue paper
PVA glue
scissors

1 Cut polystyrene trays into Christmas shapes.
2 Paint trays with powder paint. If the paint will not adhere to part of the tray, add more dishwashing liquid.
3 Glue tissue paper to the shapes. Trim when dry.

Christmas ball

you will need

polystyrene ball
foil
narrow-necked bottle
powder paint mixed with dishwashing liquid in small bowls (see page 6)
paintbrushes

1 Cover polystyrene ball with foil.
2 Set ball on bottle to prevent ball from rolling around. Paint the ball. If paint doesn't adhere add more dishwashing liquid.

glitter ball

you will need

polystyrene ball
glitter
sequins, small beads
pins (with large heads)
ribbon
PVA glue

1 Cover ball with glue. Do not use clear craft glue or spray enamel paint, which dissolve the polystyrene. Roll ball in glitter.
2 **Adult:** put sequin onto pin and insert into ball. Repeat with all sequins and beads.
3 Wrap ribbon around the ball, leaving extra length for hanging. Fasten ribbon with a pin.

'stained glass' shapes

you will need
tissue paper scraps
sheet of waxed paper
liquid starch
ribbon
hole puncher
scissors

1 Apply tissue paper scraps to
   waxed paper with liquid starch.
   Allow papers to dry.
2 Cut Christmas shapes out of the
   waxed paper. Punch a hole in the
   top of the shape, insert ribbon
   through it and hang in front of
   a light on the Christmas tree.

snowflakes

you will need
colourful squares of thin
   paper (any size)
scissors

1 Fold a square in half then fold
   in half again. Two sides of the
   square will have folds only and
   no raw edges; fold these two sides
   together to make a triangle.
2 Around outside edges of shape, cut small V shapes, half
   circles or any designs so that there is a hole left where
   the shape is cut and the edges are no longer straight.
   Unfold paper for snowflake.
   Older children can fold the squares into eighths or
   sixteenths to make a more intricate snowflake. Younger
   children may need help with cutting folded paper.

Christmas cards

Old Christmas cards make delightful
tree decorations and are easy to do.
Simply cut out designs and figures
from your favourite old cards, punch
a hole through top of cut-out, thread
a colourful ribbon through the hole
and tie it onto the tree.

pretzel ornaments

you will need
foil, about 15cm (6in) x 20cm (8in)
pretzels
red and green crinkly gift-wrapping ribbon
    or double-sided satin ribbon
PVA glue

1   Place foil on table. Arrange pretzels into a design on
    the foil so that each pretzel touches another in at
    least two places.
2   Place one large drop of glue at each point where
    pretzels touch. When joined, add another drop of glue.
3   Make sure all pretzels are touching in the glued areas.
    Leave on foil. Allow to dry overnight.
4   Remove ornament carefully from foil. Weave ribbon
    through holes. Handle the pretzel gently.

paper stars

you will need
colourful squares of thin paper,
    about 20cm (8in) square
scissors

1   Fold a square in half diagonally to make a
    triangle. Mark the centre point along fold
    (point A). Keeping first fold, fold twice more
    to make a triangle each time.
2   Fold top of triangle (point B) down as shown
    in illustration, taking care to line up folded
    edges evenly along bottom.
3   Cut away shaded area. Open paper out for
    an eight-point star. Cut a jagged line or
    cut curves for flower shapes.

wrapping presents

Paintings and prints make appealing
wrapping paper. Decorate wrapped presents
with snowflakes, which can be glued or
attached with double-sided sticky tape. Wrap
presents in foil and cover with snowflakes
(see page 115) and star shapes (see above).

advent boxes

Advent is the season before Christmas. Advent boxes are small boxes which are filled with sweets and little surprises, wrapped up and numbered from one to 24. As the countdown to Christmas begins on December 1, a present is opened each day until Christmas Eve.

you will need

24 small boxes of varying sizes
sweets, nuts, sultanas or small toys
Christmas paper scraps and children's
    paintings (for wrapping paper)
red and green crinkly
    gift-wrapping ribbon
24 adhesive labels
adhesive tape
pen
scissors

1 Fill each box with sweets, nuts or small toys.
2 Wrap each box individually with wrapping paper and secure box with tape.
3 Tie each box with ribbon and a bow. Curl loose ends of ribbon by holding ribbon firmly between thumb and back of scissors and pulling ribbon through with your free hand.
4 Write a number from one to 24 on each adhesive label. Stick a label on each box.
5 Cut 24cm (9½in) long pieces of ribbon. Tie one end onto each box. Adjust the boxes so they hang at different lengths. Take all the ribbons at the top in one hand and divide them in half. Tie halves together with a double knot and a large bow. Curl all the ends of the loose ribbons. Hang up advent boxes on the Christmas tree.

index

conversion chart

Wherever you live, you'll be able to use our projects with the help of these easy-to-follow conversions. While these conversions are approximate only, the difference between an exact and the approximate conversion of various linear, liquid and dry measures is but minimal and will not affect the results of your projects.

dry measures

metric	imperial
15g	½oz
30g	1oz
60g	2oz
90g	3oz
125g	4oz (¼lb)
155g	5oz
185g	6oz
220g	7oz
250g	8oz (½lb)
280g	9oz
315g	10oz
345g	11oz
375g	12oz (¾lb)
410g	13oz
440g	14oz
470g	15oz
500g	16oz (1lb)
750g	24oz (1½lb)
1kg	32oz (2lb)

liquid measures

metric	imperial
30ml	1 fluid oz
60ml	2 fluid oz
100ml	3 fluid oz
125ml (½ cup)	4 fluid oz
150ml	5 fluid oz (¼ pint/1 gill)
190ml	6 fluid oz
250ml (1 cup)	8 fluid oz
300ml	10 fluid oz (½ pint)
500ml	16 fluid oz
600ml	20 fluid oz (1 pint)
1000ml (1 litre)	1¾ pints

length measures

metric	imperial
1cm	½in
2cm	¾in
2.5cm	1in
5cm	2in
10cm	4in
15cm	6in
20cm	8in
25cm	10in
30cm	12in (1ft)

Editorial director *Susan Tomnay*
Designer *Mary Keep*
Sales director *Brian Cearnes*
Marketing director *Matt Dominello*
Brand manager *Renée Crea*
Production manager *Cedric Taylor*

Chief executive officer *John Alexander*
Group publisher *Pat Ingram*
Publisher *Sue Wannan*
Editorial director (AWW) *Deborah Thomas*

Produced by ACP Books, Sydney.
Printed by Dai Nippon, c/o Samhwa Printing Co
Ltd, 237-10 Kuro-Dong, Kuro-Ku, Seoul, Korea.
Published by ACP Magazines Ltd,
54 Park St, Sydney;
GPO Box 4088, Sydney, NSW 2001.
Phone +61 2 9282 8618 Fax +61 2 9267 9438
acpbooks@acpmagazines.com.au
www.acpbooks.com.au

To order books, phone 136 116.
Send recipe enquiries to:
recipeenquiries@acpmagazines.com.au

RIGHTS ENQUIRIES
Laura Bamford, Director ACP Books.
lbamford@acpmedia.co.uk

AUSTRALIA: Distributed by Network Services,
GPO Box 4088, Sydney, NSW 2001.
Phone +61 2 9282 8777 Fax +61 2 9264 3278
networkweb@networkservicescompany.com.au
UNITED KINGDOM: Distributed by Australian
Consolidated Press (UK), Moulton Park
Business Centre, Red House Rd,
Moulton Park, Northampton, NN3 6AQ.
Phone (01604) 497531 Fax (01604) 497533
books@acpmedia.co.uk
CANADA: Distributed by Whitecap Books Ltd,
351 Lynn Ave, North Vancouver, BC, V7J 2C4.
Ph: (604) 980 9852 Fax: (604) 980 8197
customerservice@whitecap.ca
www.whitecap.ca
NEW ZEALAND: Distributed by Netlink
Distribution Company, ACP Media Centre,
Cnr Fanshawe and Beaumont Streets,
Westhaven, Auckland.
PO Box 47906, Ponsonby, Auckland, NZ.
Phone (09) 366 9966 Fax 0800 277 412
ask@ndc.co.nz
SOUTH AFRICA: Distributed by PSD
Promotions, 30 Diesel Road Isando,
Gauteng Johannesburg.
PO Box 1175, Isando 1600,
Gauteng Johannesburg.
Ph: (2711) 392 6065/6/7
Fax: (2711) 392 6079/80
orders@psdprom.co.za

The Australian women's weekly
art & crafts for kids.

Includes index.
For children.
ISBN 1 86396 535 1.
1. Handicraft – Juvenile literature. 2. Creative
activities and seat work – Juvenile literature.

745.5